Successful Stock Investing

A Hunt for Wonderful Businesses

Copyright © 2016 by:
Thomas Lenz
Eggerstedtstraße 3 / 22765 Hamburg / Germany
Lenzt@gmx.net

All rights reserved. No part of this publication may be reproduced, stored in a retrieval system, or transmitted, in any form or by any means without the prior written permission of the publisher, nor be otherwise circulated in any form of binding or cover other than that in which it is published and without a similar condition being imposed on the subsequent purchaser.

Limit of Liability / Disclaimer of Warranty: While the publisher and author have used their best efforts in preparing this book, they make no representations or warranties with respect to the accuracy or completeness of the contents of this book and specifically disclaim any implied warranties of merchantability or fitness for a particular purpose. No warranty may be created or extended by sales representatives or written sales materials. The advice and strategies contained herein may not be suitable for your situation. You should consult with a professional where appropriate. Neither the publisher nor author shall be liable for any loss of profit or any other commercial damages, including but not limited to special, incidental, consequential, or other damages. Designations used by companies to distinguish their products are often claimed by trademarks. In all instances where the author or publisher is aware of a claim, the product names appear in initial capital letters. Readers, however, should contact the appropriate companies for more complete information regarding trademarks and registration.

ISBN-13: 978-1535550635
ISBN-10: 1535550635

Design of the cover and the graphics in the interior:
Gargee Gangopadhyay
Ganguly.gargee@gmail.com

Technical consultancy and marketing:
Nitin Rai

Printed in the United States of America.

*"It is not because things are difficult that we do not dare;
it is because we do not dare that they are difficult."*
(*Lucius Annaeus Seneca*)

Contents

Preface   vii

Chapters

I.   My Investment Approach   1
Know the Business, Buy Low, Hold for Long

II.   The Capitalistic Game   29
Ultimately, It's All about Dominance and Negotiation Power

III.   Economic Moats towards Intruders   55
Keeping Rivals and Substitutes out of the Game

IV.   Negotiation Power along the Value Chain   111
Dominating Customers and Suppliers

V.   The Valuation   145
Price Is What You Pay, Value Is What You Get

VI.   The Holding Period   207
Sell Never or at least for the Right Reasons

Bibliography   222

About the Author   230

List of Abbreviations   231

Preface

For me, the stock markets are one of the most fascinating Rubik's Cubes of all times. Our daily life and necessities, politics, social trends, technological developments, and many other crucial topics are debated and traded every day at the bourse. It is a vibrant place where, while investors search for the right price for a stock, emotions often dominate the events. Remarkably as well, by buying stocks, you effectively become an owner of a part of a real company with all risks and chances attached to the respective business.

To tell the truth, over the years I have been in stock investing, I have found three distinct insights about companies and stock markets to be the most intriguing, and so valuable that I actually based my whole stock investment approach on them.

First: some companies are "different" in a positive way. Having powerful and durable economics in place, such companies are able to withstand the never-stopping onslaught of competition for long periods of time. In a kind of protecting shell and being in a superior position to the other economic players, they constantly create more measurable shareholder value (i.e., cash to the shareholders) than their direct rivals or comparable industries.

This insight gave me the first reason to start with active stock investing. Due to the fact that there are

Preface

some very special or wonderful companies, consistently outperforming the average, stock picking pays off.

Second: stock markets are irrational and inefficient, at least in the short run. This is actually the second reason why active stock investing works.

We know today, not only from personal experience, but also from scientific studies, that (short-term) market inefficiencies exist. Behavioural finance, one field of finance that proposes psychology-based theories to explain stock market anomalies, delivers a bunch of solid reasons and empirically proven insights why market inefficiencies temporarily occur – and will do so in the future. In the short term, stock markets are ruled by human beings and their emotions. Rumours, unskilled guessing, feelings like fear and greed, cheap money flying around – all these things make the daily stock exchange look like a madhouse sometimes; money just makes most people behave irrationally and act in a myopic way. With that, market inefficiency seems to be irreversibly connected with the human nature.

The resulting noise and volatility at the daily bourse are what many investors interpret as a threat or risk, but this conclusion is not correct. Markets need to undergo these ups and downs in order to find finally the fair price of a stock. All news and views get discussed and weighted by the involved market participants. Some information or opinions are very hard to digest, and some attached feelings are too extreme to get over them easily. Only in the long run, opinions and emotions will lose their dominating influence. Then, at some point in the future, stock markets and all protagonists start to take a rational view on the relevant facts that really drive cash flows and resulting value. It often requires quite some time until the weighting process comes to a proper result. In the end, the market mechanisms at work find the fair price that equals the intrinsic or true value of a stock.

An intelligent investor knows about the necessity of noise and volatility. And he or she does not perceive that as a kind of risk in the stock investment process. **Investment risk** for him or her is solely the probability to lose money with a stock position. Investment risk and investment return are actually like the two sides of the same coin. Just as the chance in stock investing lies in earning money,[1] the risk in stock investing lies in losing money – it is as simple as that.

But it is the noise and volatility at the daily markets that make stock prices drop sometimes below their intrinsic or true value. Therefore, the intelligent investor appreciates the ups and downs; it gives him or her the opportunity to buy value at a cheap price. All he or she has to do is to stoically wait till the stock markets also get it right, and the gap between price and value closes again.

Third: even small investment amounts can accumulate at the stock exchange to a large amount of wealth over time. All you need is consistency and

---

[1] In a business-like manner, the **investment return** is the sum of cash flows that an equity investor is able to obtain over time from his or her stake in a company. These cash flows can come in the form of rising stock prices, dividend payments, proceeds from buyback programs, and any other pay-outs that a firm might make to its owners.

Preface

patience in order to benefit from one of the most amazing and powerful phenomenon in financial mathematics – the **compound interest effect**.

Quite frankly, this book will not tell you the secret of how to quickly get rich by juggling stocks. But what it gives you is a fundamental and robust framework for successful stock investing. As I depict, basically, a classic buy-and-hold strategy, I will explain to you, step by step and in detail, what successful stock investing is finally about.

My investment approach is for sure not the only valid method for investing in stocks, but it is the one that has worked best for me over the last years, no matter how the overall stock markets were doing. In this book, I describe the ins and outs of my investment philosophy, which can be used by you to identify wonderful businesses at reasonable prices in order to build up a resilient, safe, and outperforming stock portfolio.

I love to watch the capitalistic game and to understand how the value creation processes of businesses function. For me, it is this never-ending learning experience and the constant intellectual challenge that genuinely adds zest to stock investing; it would be great if I could convey a little bit of my passion via this book to you.

I. My Investment Approach

Know the Business, Buy Low, Hold for Long

As introduced before, my investment approach is established on only three pivotal comprehensions: some businesses are more resilient and profitable than others, the markets are solely efficient in the long run, and the compound interest effect makes your stock portfolio grow exponentially over time.

Consequently, my investment approach can be broken down into just three steps:

1. Identify wonderful businesses that can safely generate above-average profits for many years

2. Wait till the shares of those businesses trade for less than their intrinsic (i.e., fair) value and buy then

3. Keep those shares for many years unless and until there are some very good reasons to sell

At first glance, my methodology to invest in stocks is pretty straightforward - know the business, buy low, hold for long. But it takes thorough understanding of the business, deep insight about the short-term drivers of the stock exchange, and quite a bit of staying power (i.e., mental balance); these are the areas where the challenges for an investor come from.

Let me now explain each of the listed steps a little bit to give you a solid overview. Based on that, material aspects in this approach will be elaborated in much more detail later in separate chapters. All information and explanations together then will finally give you a working and dependable compass for your successful stock investments in practice.

Step One

If you can do this, you will already be ahead of many investors. The identification of companies or industries with outstanding quality characteristics is the most complex and momentous task in stock investing. But why is it of such paramount importance for an investor to spot businesses with long-term favourable economics?

Well, at the core, stock investing is about earning money. And, of course, this can be done best with companies or industries that are profitable and, more importantly, that do well over long periods of time. Such single companies or industries are the wealth-building machines that should populate your portfolio. Your odds to be successful as a stock investor will be much higher if you put your money in wonderful firms or industries with steadfast economics and reliable prospects.

For example, think about a world-class company like PepsiCo, the legendary food, snacks, and drinks maker. Although it has faced intense competitive pressure for many years, this undertaking is still extremely profitable and cranks out very high returns on invested capital.[2] Maybe it is merely very lucky or, more likely, has some special characteristics that most other companies lack.

A **wonderful business** embodies essentially all the following characteristics:

> ➢ It faces a crucial customer need as well as a strong and (in the best-case scenario) rising customer demand
> ➢ It supplies an easy value proposition via a good business model
> ➢ It has competitive advantages over all the other economic players in the capitalistic game

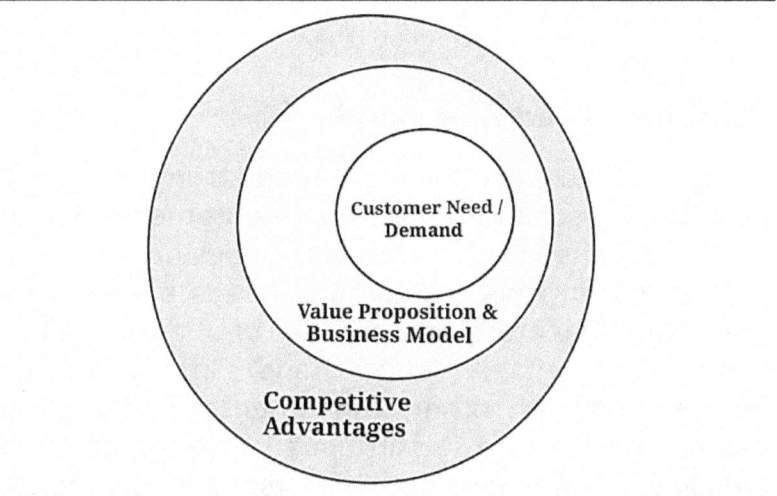

Exhibit 1 **A Wonderful Business**

---

[2] Profitability in the context of this book is primarily measured with the **return on invested capital** (**ROIC**) concept. ROIC is the (net) operating profit of the company, divided by its (average) invested capital (i.e., operating assets).

My Investment Approach

You can express it also in one sentence: a wonderful business is a well-designed and low-risk business model around a crucial customer need and a strong, at least steady, customer demand, safeguarded and strengthened by competitive advantages.

To be honest with you, there are very few businesses that meet all these criteria. Actually, many do not even fulfil one of these criteria. The reality is that every business has, of course, its strengths, weaknesses, opportunities, and threats.

But that is not per se bad news for you anymore. With the criteria mentioned above, you have from now on a dependable orientation guide to find the most promising companies.

Customer Need / Demand

A crucial need as well as a related strong and (in the best-case scenario) rising customer demand demarcate the core of a wonderful business.

Apart from this, customers' needs and demands are fundamental elements of the industry environment itself and stand in a dynamic interrelation with other, fundamental elements like technology or the institutional framework of an industry. I will explain the concept of industry environment and the role of individuals' needs and demands in this setting in more detail in the next chapter.

A strong and lasting customer demand results, spring-fed and bounded by a certain ability of the customers to pay, in the first place in ample and predictable revenue streams, the mainstay of a high and durable ROIC.

A customer need is to be labelled crucial or vital if it is of paramount importance from the individual customer's viewpoint and, in extreme, to be satisfied on a daily basis. Ultimately, you as an investor must understand the product or service and its true value in the eyes of the customers; that value is what the customers finally and largely pay for. It has to become clear to you what kind of customers have actually what need, how much, how often, and for what final reason.

Maslow's hierarchy of needs as a psychological concept might give a good indication or guideline for the customers' needs and the resulting demands, something I will also elaborate in the next chapter a little bit more.

But in the end, it will be you who has to apply logic, life experience, and a bit of your business sense to determine the quality and potential development of a certain customer demand.

Nutrition might be, at first glance, a very classic example for an essential customer need, likely fitting to the fundament of Maslow's hierarchy of needs. The resulting demand is also quite frequent in nature, having the potential to create a day-to-day business for many undertakings.

But be careful. Nutrition might be a primary need for every individual every day. Nevertheless, such a basic requirement can also change the way it is expressed in concrete demands. Actually, eating and drinking are likely too broad to be a manifest customer demand from an investor's perspective.

My Investment Approach

These days, people are starting to put more emphasis on aspects like health and sustainability. With this social trend coming up more and more, both the requested quality of food and beverages as well as the way they are produced is altered.

Inevitably, even nutrition, as such a basic need, is undergoing deep transformations over time. And although human beings will still for sure have a metabolism tomorrow, structural trends can notably change the way food and beverages are valued and finally demanded by individuals.

In addition, be careful of what customer need you are essentially looking at. In business-to-business relations, a customer need is much clearer and often just related to efficiency or productivity. The product or service of the providing company is only demanded as an input factor by other firms if it really creates a value in money terms.

And these receiving companies in turn have, of course, their own customers. All the way down the value chain, there are finally the end consumers that are driven by their needs described with the Maslow hierarchy. These are the needs that ultimately drive all demands along the complete value chain.

Please make sure that you have understood the value chain as a whole, from the very origin to the actual (end) consumption. It will help you tremendously to estimate the current status and the future prospects of a single company on that total value chain.

In a nutshell and as mentioned earlier, you as the investor have to apply your own logic and life experience to get a clear view on this chief domain.

Unfortunately, there is no precise formula or rule of thumb that can help you to estimate the importance and development of a customer demand. You can't assess the quality and prospects of a customer demand only by analysing financial statements and statistics. It is more – and it is all your call as an investor. But at the end of the day, it is about understanding people and their actual needs, accompanied by some business acumen. It is about realising the drivers of everybody's daily lives and linking them to the individuals' resulting demands.

And when thinking about the potential developments of demands, you should think in decades rather than only in months or single years. Secular trends like globalization of production and trade, growing and aging of the world population, international security, reliable energy supply, Internet and digitalisation or ecologic sustainability arise slowly at the beginning but can awaken crucial customer needs over time and represent the strong demands of generations to come.

Being interested in people, society, nature, politics, technology, economy, or - in one word - life, is an irreplaceable character trait in order to be good at this central task of identifying crucial needs and strong demands. All these aspects of life continuously change and impact each other, sometimes quite significantly and swiftly.

With that, customer needs and the corresponding demands undergo changes over time. By keeping track of the big stories, you will see such changes, or opportunities and threats from an investor's perspective, before the crowd will.

Value Proposition and Business Model

Generally, a customer demand is satisfied by a firm via a tailor-made, neatly fitting value proposition and a related business model.

A **value proposition** is an offer or a promise of a company to its customers that their demands will be met in a certain way at a certain price in exchange; by that, the firm creates **customer value**.

The **business model** is the distinct blueprint, set up by the firm's leadership in order to deliver the value proposition to the customer. The business model describes a company's core plan to generate customer value in exchange for money from its customers, expressed in the form of revenues. It states how the firm will make sufficient economic value for itself by converting inputs like operating assets, technology, raw materials, and labour into outputs or customer value; in short, the business model describes how the company is planning to earn money from its operations.

The ROIC is the financial reflection of that business model and the inherent value proposition.

As investors, we are hunting for an easy value proposition delivered by a proper business model, embedded in a good strategy. Because some strategies are different from others, it is important to understand the basic elements of a "good" one; I will describe the concept of a good strategy in the next chapter, too.

A value proposition is "easy" if the overall risk for the providing firm to incur losses during the value creation process is structurally low and / or can be effectively mitigated with a good strategy.

As a matter of principle, there are two sources and, with that, categories of risk for a company while conducting its business. Inside an undertaking, the internal value creation process itself causes **operational risks**. But a company is also affected from the outside surroundings by externally given factors. The industry environment and its elements represent **business drivers** to a company that can bring **business risks** to it.

Both operational and business risks can be further classified concerning the frequency of an adverse event, the significance of the potential impact, and its likelihood. A reasonable and complete classification enables a company to set up a working risk management strategy. Generally, risks can be (deliberately) tolerated, shared (e.g., via an insurance), or actively mitigated via proper management action. Which risk management plan will work best always depends on the nature of risk on the one hand and the combination of frequency, significance, and likelihood on the other hand. Just like the value proposition itself, each accompanied risk calls for a tailor-made strategy from management too.

Operational risks represent the possibility of losses from inadequate or failed internal procedures, systems, and policies. They are the risks a firm needs to take when it attempts to operate within a given business field or industry.

Operational risks will change from industry to industry, and that structural aspect has to be taken into consideration by you when doing an investment analysis about a firm. Operational risks affect client satisfaction, reputation, and finally shareholder value, all while increasing business uncertainty.

Unfortunately, operational risks can't be perfectly laid off, meaning that as long as people, systems, and processes remain imperfect, operational risks can't be fully eliminated. Nevertheless, operational risks can be mitigated and answered with operational excellence, a part of strategy that I will also explain in more detail in the next chapter.

The value creation processes of a wonderful business are already structurally easy or, in other words, straightforward and manageable from a risk perspective. From just looking at the whole transformation process, from the required input over the actual making to the final delivery, it's clear some products or services naturally are definitely not complex and hence are uncomplicated to make. And if related operating processes can be excellently run by the firm's management via appropriate and reliable people, systems, and policies, the probability that something goes really wrong during the value creation can be further reduced to a considerable extent. Indicators for a low-risk process landscape can be low accident rates and the lack of negative incidents like product recalls, plant shutdowns, fires, and other materialised risks in the past.

Besides complexity, time is another structural risk element in a value creation process. The faster the product or service is finalised by the firm and received by the customer, the lower the risk from the firm's side and the sooner revenues can be booked.

Therefore, the whole value creation process of a wonderful business does not take much time by nature. The value creation process is also in this regard easy; in the best-case scenario, good process management just expedites the entire procedure.

Let us turn now to the category of external / business risks. By threatening a company from the outside, business risks stand for the likelihood of inadequate profits or even losses for a company due to adverse changes of the externally given business drivers.

The ultimate risk is that the customer demand, the central element of any industry, changes or even vanishes. That's why it is of cardinal importance for an investor to be sure about the stability and strength of a customer need and the resulting demand.

But independent from the customer demand itself, the other structural elements of an industry can also change and hence directly affect a company's value proposition and respective business model in a negative way.

What input in terms of operational assets does the company require to do its business? How do the markets for these operational assets work? How many people does the company require to handle its operations? Where do these people come from, what educational background do they have to have, and how scarce are they on the labour market? What kind of raw material is needed for the end products, and how is the situation in the related markets? Where does the value creation process in general take place? In which geographic areas is the company doing its main business? Are they politically safe? Does a business have revenues, costs, and investments in the same currency? Will a shift in the value of a particular currency affect the company's profitability positively or negatively?

My Investment Approach

Internet, digitalisation, 3-D printing, genetic engineering, renewable energies – can the company benefit from an upcoming technologic trend, or does a game-changing technology threaten the whole business model of the company you are looking at? Digitalisation, to pick one as an example, has the potential to strengthen or destroy the business models of many existing entities just by enhancing information flows over the whole value chain. Furthermore, digitalisation will create new business opportunities and markets which in turn can threaten the industries we know today.

All such questions and related answers will help you to understand the company and the structural setting in which it is doing its business. Every business driver, with all the chances and risks attached to it, matters for you as an investor. It is indispensable for an investor to know how a company is positioned in a certain market structure and what strategy it follows in order to exploit the opportunities while managing the risks.

This exercise is explicitly not about precisely estimating or quantifying all these external factors; this is not workable anyway. But as an investor, you need to logically comprehend the complete composition and all related elements of the revenues, operating costs and assets - hence, ROIC - and all potential impacts from the main business drivers. Only after such thorough analysis will the picture of the business you are interested in become complete.

A favourable development in one business driver might be the reason for you to see a good investment opportunity right ahead - fair enough. Nevertheless, as a cautious investor, you should first and foremost focus on the threats or business risks to the company you are scrutinising.

This is the part where things can really go wrong in the stock investment process. The issue stems from the **confirmation bias**: the tendency of people to see only the information that is compatible with their existing theories and to filter out any new information that contradicts their prevailing views. In order to fight the confirmation bias (i.e., to prevent becoming blind to disconfirming evidence), you should force yourself and actively search for (external) reasons not to undertake a particular investment.

Besides the already-mentioned business drivers, business risks can also stem from various other areas - for instance, swings in economic cycles, changes in governmental regulations (e.g., legislation, subsidies, quotas), climate (i.e., weather), or even terrorism. The business risks from swings in economic cycles depend largely on the nature of the customer value a firm offers. The more crucial (i.e., essential and frequent) the underlying customer needs, the less the resulting demands as well as the firm's overall business performance will get negatively affected by a general downturn in the economy.

Especially worthwhile to mention are significant business risks that can't be mitigated by a firm's management via a good risk management strategy and respective operating processes.

Terrorism is such a business risk. Terrorism panics people, which is its demonic intention, and due to that, a terroristic attack on one airline directly hurts the business of all peers in the industry. Hotel chains, travel agencies, airlines – the whole tourist and travel industry suffers if people prefer to stay at their safe homes rather than to go on a private vacation or a business trip. But such risks are inherent in these businesses and are hence structural in nature. In case a company still wants to be in a business with such a risk profile, the only alternatives left from a risk management perspective then are either moderating via an insurance cover, if possible, or just tolerating. It is such massive, non-manageable risks like potential terroristic attacks you should sidestep as an investor.

Epidemics or pandemic diseases like the Ebola virus or the new Zika virus also fall in this category of extremely disruptive business risks. Some industries are structurally threatened by colossal risks from the outside that neither can be tamed with operational measures nor can be insured. Classic risk management strategies simply do not function in some cases.

The exact frequency and likelihood of the negative events do not matter here. Such risks can and will materialise at some unknown point in time for which neither a company nor you can prepare. And if the unpleasant event happens, it will hit the company, and thus your investment, hard.

Keeping away from trouble is one vital element of my investment approach. Therefore, without even trying to exactly quantify the likelihood and frequency of the negative external events, which is anyway very difficult (i.e., near to impossible), please do not invest in industries and companies that expose structurally a high-impact profile as described.[3]

Competitive Advantages

As a matter of fact, competitive advantages are the forces that put a company in an enhanced position to bargain with customers and suppliers, while holding rivals and substitutes out of the game. Due to competitive advantages, a wonderful business has enhanced **negotiation power** at constant levels and, with that, a well-fortified and profitable position on the **competitive field**. Like the customer need / demand and the value proposition / business model, the competitive advantages also find their expression in a firm's ROIC.

Just as moats around medieval castles kept the opposition at bay, economic moats protect the high ROIC enjoyed by the respective companies or industries against competitive pressure from peers and substitutes.[4]

---

[3] The **neglect of probability**, a type of cognitive bias, is a general tendency of individuals to completely disregard probabilities for absolutes when evaluating situations under uncertainty and is one simple way in which people regularly violate the normative rules for decision making. Small probabilities, no matter what the magnitude of the potential outcome would be, are typically either not taken into account at all or hugely overrated; the continuum between the extremes is ignored. Daniel Kahneman, *Thinking, Fast and Slow* (London: Penguin Books, 2012).

[4] Lawrence A. Cunningham, *The Essays of Warren Buffet: Lessons for Investors and Managers*. 4th ed. (Singapore: John Wiley & Sons Singapore, 2014).

Such "indirect" competitive advantages or barriers to entry enhance the negotiation power of some companies or industries towards the customers and suppliers by keeping rivals and substitutes away from interfering with the actual business.

Competitive advantages directly along the value chain have to be seen separately. Such "direct" competitive advantages enhance the negotiation power of the firm straight towards its customers and suppliers. But exactly like the "indirect" ones, competitive advantages directly working along the value chain also rest in both at the same time: the structure of an industry and a firm's strategy.

Although the impact of management can significantly vary, depending on the given parameters in a business, it is always a synthesis of both industry environment and strategy by which a firm can get into a dominant position within the capitalistic game. I will tackle this critical aspect as well in the next chapter.

The leading question for you as an investor is: "How does a company conquer and defend its turf towards all the other economic players on the competitive field?"

Competitive advantages clearly are far more than just the icing on the cake – they are a vital part of a wonderful business and hence my investment approach.

Competitive advantages are of such principal importance for the overall financial performance of a company and, decisively, for the definition of a wonderful business that I actually dedicated the next three chapters in this book to them.

Step Two

If investing were as straightforward as just identifying wonderful companies, making money in the stock market would already be a lot easier – and this investment approach would have solely two steps. But the reality is that the price you pay for a stock is critically important to your overall investment success. You must have an idea about the right price or true value of a stock because the price at which you step into a certain stock directly determines your investment return. Even the finest stock will burden your portfolio's performance if you pay too much for it. And investment risk comes not only from misunderstanding the business and its drivers, but also just from losing money by paying too much for what you get.

In financial economics, the **efficient market hypothesis** (**EMH**) states that stock prices fully reflect all available information, and that newly popping up information is immediately translated into the quotations. In the strong form of the EMH, stock prices do entail not only all publicly accessible information but also all private "insider" information. With that, stocks continuously trade at their intrinsic values, which (theoretically) makes it impossible for investors to either purchase undervalued stocks or sell stocks for inflated prices.

Well, that might hold true, but only on average and at long sight. Stock prices can't always trade at efficient or perfectly rational levels because the respective market is ultimately made by human beings. The "market" is an intellectual construct, encompassing in reality an immeasurable number of individuals, all with their own skills, motivations and character traits. **Behavioural finance** as a scientific concept is the link between the short-term inefficiency and the long-term efficiency of stock markets. Behavioural finance explains and hence heals the inconsistency of the EMH concept in the short run by bringing human psychology into the picture. For this reason, behavioural finance does not contradict the EMH but complements it.

The point of contention, in my view, is more about how long it takes the stock markets to get it right, not if there are actually inefficient stock prices or investment opportunities, from time to time. More specific, the question is how long it takes the market participants to incorporate new information with all its facets and aftermaths into the stock prices. The EMH says that the market bakes in all information into the stock prices in seconds.

But inarguably, once fresh information arrives, there is often quite a time lag as the whole process needs rational thoughts and action from investors in order to bring stock prices to efficient levels again.

The reasonable assumption that there is in the end an efficient market state actually implies that there must be also an inefficient state of that market at some point in time as the efficient equilibrium of stock prices constantly changes. The way from one equilibrium to the next must be bridged by someone who is the first at detecting the market inefficiency and acts accordingly. Because the markets are inefficient in the short term to middle term but efficient in the long run, investing in single stocks economically makes sense.

Otherwise, you will behave like the professor of finance who believes only in the EMH. As he is taking a walk one day with one of his students, the student suddenly spots a hundred-dollar bill right on the sideway. The student wants to collect it, but the professor holds him back and says: "Do not try; there is nothing. If there were a hundred-dollar bill just lying on the street, someone would have picked it up already."

So although in the long-term equilibrium there might be no chances for a bargain, as all information is properly weighted and incorporated into the stock prices, the way from one efficient state to another leads in the short run to investment opportunities for the attentive investor who sees an undervalued stock first.

The root cause behind the often hampered and lengthy adjustment process from the old equilibrium stock price to a new one is, as mentioned already, human psychology. Feelings and emotions make prices in the short run. People are often not behaving rationally – this is a fact and not an assumption. Especially when faced with new information that requires a hard decision or a strong reaction, individuals regularly tend to behave not logically but emotionally, at least in the short view. It takes time to think about all consequences and to make sensible decisions when a new, material event occurs.

Unfortunately, Mother Nature gave us instinct to speed up our reactions, which all too often results in cognitive errors and heuristics and hence wrong decisions in financial matters. People also tend to seek advice from others to make their decisions. And the bigger and more significant a matter and the required move, the more people follow the crowd as this feels safer for each of them – the "classic" herding behaviour. It is especially this social or cognitive behaviour of human beings that habitually creates significant deviations between a stock's price and its true value for quite some time, making active stock picking a winning investment approach.[5] And apart from the lemming-like herding behaviour, there are other barriers to logic that stop people again and again from behaving in a rational manner, repeating patterns through the generations and over the centuries.

Many people at the bourse regularly are **anchoring** their investment decisions to sometimes totally uncorrelated and hence irrelevant figures. In addition and as mentioned a little earlier, some investors do selective filtering and pay highest attention to information that supports their investment thesis while ignoring the rest. By just looking at the information that suits them best, such individuals are basically oversimplifying the matters, mixing up cause and effect, and make bad decisions at the end.

Hindsight bias tends to occur in situations where a person believes, after the fact, that the onset of a particular event could have been reasonably predicted. **Overconfidence** fits into the same

---

[5] To learn more about the **herd behaviour effect** and related **social proof bias**, please see Rolf Dobelli, *The Art of Thinking Clearly* (London: Sceptre, 2013). Richard H. Thaler and Cass R. Sunstein, *Nudge: Improving Decisions about Health, Wealth, and Happiness* (New York: Penguin Books, 2009).

category and implies an exaggerated optimistic assessment of one's own knowledge or control over a situation. Please clearly see that there is more than a fine line between (solid) confidence and (arrogant) overconfidence, which you should never cross. Due to both, hindsight bias as well as overconfidence, people are willing to take more (non-understood) risks and trade unnecessarily often.

Gambler's fallacy. This well-known but inglorious effect in principle describes individuals erroneously believing that the onset of a certain random event is less likely to happen following another particular event or series of events. The reason for this stems from a lack of understanding how statistics works. In case of independent events, the odds of any specific outcome happening on the next chance remains the same regardless of what preceded it. So stock prices can indeed drop in series; in the worst case, for good reasons and without a bottom. Once investors have fallen prey to it on the trading floor, the gambler's fallacy can tempt them to catch falling knives.

Another example is (harsh) **overreaction** in case of unanticipated events. And last but not least – the **prospect theory** or **loss aversion** with the accompanied **disposition effect**. All these cognitive biases and heuristics systematically create temporary inconsistencies between the price and the intrinsic value of a stock, ultimately due to human nature.[6]

---

[6] Daniel Kahneman, *Thinking, Fast and Slow* (London: Penguin Books, 2012). Terry Burnham and Jay Phelan, *Mean Genes* (New York: Penguin Books, 2001). Nassim Nicholas Taleb, *Fooled by Randomness: The Hidden Role of Chance in Life and in the Markets* (London: Penguin Books, 2007).

In conclusion, the exercise of estimating the value of a company's share is a must as it enables you to buy stocks at prices less than their true potential, pushing and safeguarding your investment success.

Recognising when others are in thrall to these systematic errors will give you a strong action signal. Seek buying opportunities when the others start to panic and stay away from the stock market when the others become too greedy. In addition, being aware of the threat from your personal human errors will enable you to change course before lasting damage is done to your own stock portfolio.

There is no successful stock investing without the right buy, no matter how scrupulous your study of the wonderful business might have been. But the right buy always comes after the initially done analysis, as this investment approach is not about chasing cheap stocks that might have a chance to bounce back from their lows but about wonderful stocks at reasonable prices. But what is a company worth anyway? What is "value" in the context of stock investing, and what drives it? Simple questions – simple answers. A company's (equity) value is the sum of all the future cash flows that will be generated by an undertaking for the respective shareholders (i.e., stock investors), discounted back to the present;[7] that's it.

Yet stock valuation is a kind of funny thing. Everyone knows quite well what to pay for a car or a house and would sacrifice quite some time and effort in order to save some percentages on such buy. But when it comes to stocks, most people and even

---

[7] Excess cash of today, not needed to run the operations or to defend the firm's competitive position, can also be paid out as value to the investors.

professional investors have only a vague idea of the potential value of a business. The reason for this is again straightforward – valuing stocks is hard, as the many relevant parameters are pretty uncertain. Every company and its business model is slightly different from other firms even in the same industry, which makes comparison tough. Risks, return on capital, strength and duration of competitive advantages, and a host of other vague factors all drive the value of a business. Moreover, the value of a company is directly tied to its future financial performance such as the strength and the growth rate of the revenues, which are unknown. That's why investors can obviously make only some educated guesses. For these reasons, most people focus on the information that is easily attainable about stocks (i.e., their market price) rather than the information that is harder to obtain (i.e., their business values).

This uncertainty and complexity in valuation is the bad news, as it can make this exercise tricky and risky. The good news for you is that you do not need to know the precise value of a company before buying its shares. All you have to know is that the current market price is lower than the most likely value of that company.

That may sound pretty simplistic for now, but I will elaborate later in a separate chapter that, essentially, estimating a proper buying price for a stock is about breaking down the capital return ratios of a company into their fundamentals and examining these factors with your knowledge about the whole business in the background. After that, based on your understanding and accompanied by your personal appetite for risk and return, a set of valuation techniques can be used

My Investment Approach

in order to determine a fair stock price in your eyes, for which you just need to patiently wait.

As a matter of principle, you need to be reasonably sure that there is more money coming out of your stock investment via dividends, share repurchases, and capital appreciation than you originally paid for. That way, you follow the first and most important ground rule in stock investing: never lose money. Your prime goal must be to get your initially invested money back as quickly and securely as possible from the company you own. Everything on top comes for you as a positive investment return then.

So the key take-away for the start is that you do not have to know exactly what the future will bring. You are just asked to know if the determining factors within the market price are too conservative or too optimistic in your opinion and act accordingly. Right at this point, your logic and understanding about the business and its value drivers is in strong demand. Right here, you can apply your knowledge gained in step one. Do not speculate but invest, meaning that you need to know the company's business inside out, estimate long-term prospects, and should not pay for too-rosy outlooks.

If you have done a good job during the first step of my investment approach, you will be able to challenge the expectations of all other market participants, which are expressed in the stock's market price and the underlying input parameters. Once you catch sight of a wonderful stock that is, according to you, not adequately honoured by the market – buy and put it with confidence into your portfolio.

Step Three

Following the first two steps of my investment approach will likely result already in solid returns for you over time. So if you can identify companies that have, in the ideal situation, all attributes of a wonderful business, and you can purchase their shares at reasonable prices, you will build a great portfolio that will enormously improve your odds of doing well at the bourse.

But along with a correct investment analysis and a proper buying price, the holding period and the right selling price also logically determine the overall investment success.

You can do a brilliant analysis and make a clever purchase decision. But selling at the wrong point in time for the wrong reasons can reduce your overall performance significantly. Or expressed positively – smart selling means even better and safer returns.

At first sight, stocks suggest, due to the easy interchangeability via the bourse on a daily basis, that they are short-term investments in nature. But this is a crass misconception of many people. As a stock owner, you become actually one of the owners of a real company and the business behind it.

A stock investment is in fact a very long-term commitment to a company. And as a stock owner you need to expose the same qualities like an entrepreneur who founds and leads a firm in order to emerge victorious in the capitalistic game. Businesses and values are not built overnight; good things need time and accrue only over years. The right vision,

My Investment Approach

resoluteness, and stamina are prerequisites in order to be successful with a venture. Thereby, stock investments become actually one of the most long-term investments available as asset class, comparable in this respect, for instance, with real estate.

In any case, the stock exchange will need some time to see the true value of the stock too. So you will have to show some patience anyway until the gap between your buying price and the intrinsic value of the stock closes.

But of course, holding periods are not supposed to be infinite either. For this, stock investing can also be understood as a kind of cycle. At some point in time, money in hand was put into a promising investment opportunity. And after a long while for a (hopefully) good reason, it is time to return that investment again into mammon.

When the investment has been transferred back into money, the game you once started is over. You are suddenly rid of the risks and solicitudes attached to stocks and can enjoy the gained money to the full, but you also lost the chances inherent in the sold stocks and the benefit of the compound interest effect, which does pure magic in top quality stocks over longer periods of time.

In addition to that, by selling, you expose your stock portfolio to taxes and related transaction costs, which directly lowers your overall investment return and weakens the future potential of the mentioned compound interest effect.

Due to all that, the act of selling must be accepted as an integral and important part of the stock investment process but should be based on the right motives. The main reasons for smart selling will be elaborated in a separate chapter at the very end of this book.

Investment Return Up, Investment Risk Down

Just to make it as clear as crystal to you: following each step of my investment approach will actually help you to enhance your investment return and to mitigate your investment risk at the same time.

Focussing only on wonderful businesses - cash-producing powerhouses with durable economics and reliable prospects - significantly increases your chances to do well with your stock portfolio. Due to their superior characteristics, wonderful businesses do really fine over time and do not surprise in a negative way.

Understanding and estimating a reasonable price for the respective stock ensures then that you do not pay too much for what you get, especially for growth. Furthermore, a solid valuation exercise results in a proper price basis with limited downside risk and maximum upside potential.

Finally, holding a stock for a long time saves taxes and transaction fees but more important, brings out the best of the magical compounding effect. And the longer you actually hold your stake in a company, the lower your investment risk, because at some point in time, your stock position has earned back what you originally paid for it.

My Investment Approach

II. The Capitalistic Game

Ultimately, It's All about Dominance and Negotiation Power

The basic purpose of every company in the capitalistic system is to make profits by creating a value for its customers in exchange for money. This can generally be done either by production (i.e., transforming various kinds of inputs into physical outputs) or by providing services. A firm creates value for itself if the revenues earned exceed the costs incurred and the investments made.

But this value creation process does not happen in an empty space. The economic environment a firm is acting in is based on and framed by externally given parameters. And within this structural setting or marketplace, value creation does not translate automatically into profits for the respective firm. The surplus of revenues over the (firm's) costs and investments is finally determined by the invisible forces of competition.

Think about values that come from products such as cocoa or coffee. Yes, apparently pretty plain farm products, but likely forever high in consumer's demand because of the endless ways to process, perfect, and enjoy them. Yet not everybody who works on the respective total value chains, from the plantation down to the end consumer, will be able to earn enough for a proper living. Actually, some **economic players** often suffer, while others constantly take very good money home, and customers consume the delicate end products with relish at cheap prices.

To comprehend this, **competition** in turn must be understood as much more than just the direct interrelation between the firm and its customers or a sole contest between rivals about who makes the sale (i.e., who is the "best" at creating the customer value).

No, competition is a broader struggle over profits, a tug-of-war between many different parties about who will capture the bulk of the total value a market generates and who earns the highest profits compared to all others on the competitive field.

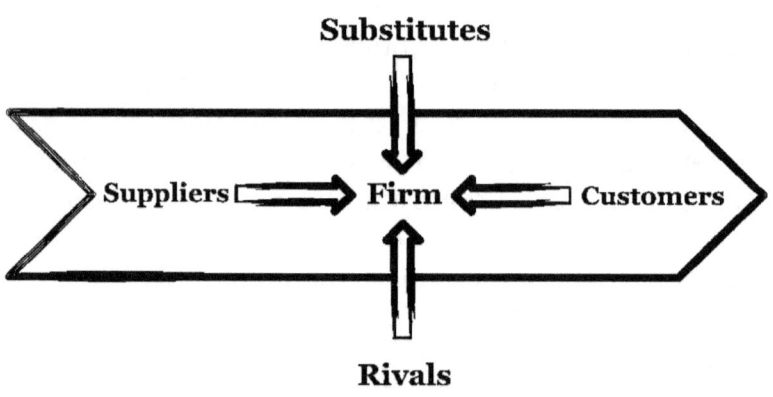

Exhibit 2.1 **The Competitive Field - Pressure from All Sides**

Of course, companies fight for profits with their existing rivals. These are the first who can disturb a firm's business with its customers. But companies are also directly engaged in a struggle for profits with their customers, who would always be happier to pay less and get more. They compete with their suppliers, who would always be happier to get paid more and deliver less. They battle against other producers, who make products that could, at a pinch, be substituted for their own. And they contend with potential, completely new rivals, because even the threat of such trespassers places limits on how much they can charge their customers.

These all are the economic players or **competitive forces** that populate the competitive field of every company.[8]

It might be noted right here that the different roles in the capitalistic game are sometimes neither easily defined nor cut in stone. For instance, the distinction between a rival and a substitute can be a tough call. Both satisfy the same customer need / demand and hence could be merged from that point of view in just one category: **intruders**. Also, the roles of customers and suppliers can change over time. Customers can become a firm's peer via backwards integration under some circumstances, and suppliers can do so by integrating forward.

Nevertheless, a general competitive analysis, based on the definition of certain stereotypes of competitive forces, has been proven to be useful in order to seize the overall competitive situation in an industry and the effects from competition on profitability.[9]

---

[8] Joan Magretta, *Understanding Michael Porter: The Essential Guide to Competition and Strategy* (Boston: Harvard Business Review Press, 2012). Michael E. Porter, *Competitive Advantage: Creating and Sustaining Superior Performance* (New York: Free Press, 2004).

[9] Robert E. Hoskisson, Michael A. Hitt, and R. Duane Ireland, *Competing for Advantage* (Mason, Ohio: Thomson South-Western, 2004).

Looking then at any given competitive field, we can say that the profits earned by an incumbent firm are determined by three fundamental aspects:

- ➢ The (relative) value of the firm's product or service for the customers[10]
- ➢ The bargaining power of the incumbent firm directly along the value chain towards customers and suppliers
- ➢ The impact from (potential and existing) rivals as well as substitutes from the "outside" on the incumbent firm's direct bargaining power along the value chain

Ultimately, it is the economic player in the most dominant position in relation to all others within the capitalistic game who takes the biggest possible gain home. Due to this very reason, every company first and foremost aims to get into a superior negotiation position towards its customers and suppliers while vigorously keeping its rivals and substitutes at bay.

Such **dominance** (i.e., negotiation power) sometimes comes from a natural limitation of physical production resources. The respective owning company is then structurally in an excellent position, uttermost in a monopolistic position, to bargain exclusively with the customer side.

---

[10] Looking from the demand side, the price (i.e., value) of a product or service is determined by the customers' willingness and ability to pay. The more essential a firm's product or service is and the more frequently customers require it, the higher the general willingness of customers to pay. Urgency and frequency of the customers' demands go hand in hand with the true nature of their underlying needs, limited of course by the customers' fixed budgets and other spending requirements.

With that, it is the firm being in possession of the essentially needed and (relatively) scarce value creation resource that will be in the most powerful bargaining position directly towards the customers in order to extract the most value in the form of cash profits. Interestingly and due to that, a product or service does not have to be complicated or cutting edge in order to be high in price (i.e., value) and hence highly profitable for the producing or providing firm. It is most often a very easy and basic customer value that results in remarkable profits for the respective company.

But the possession of a naturally limited production resource is just one measure that can create superiority for a product or service and, with that, an advantaged position for the company as such on the competitive ground. There are also other structural circumstances and distinct management strategies possible that can bring a firm in a (more) exclusive and thereby dominating role in the capitalistic game as a whole. Such **competitive advantages** are then the genuine reason for enhanced dominance of the incumbent firm towards all the other economic forces, superior negotiation power towards customers as well as suppliers, and the true source of a company's enhanced profitability. In other words, competitive advantages are the antidote to the pressure on a company's profitability in the capitalistic game.

The Capitalistic Game

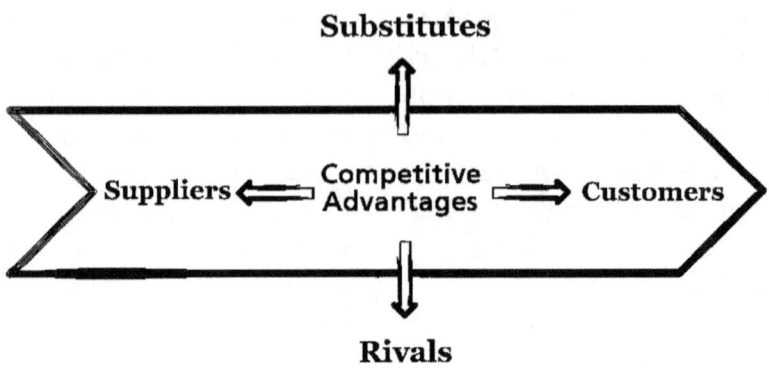

Exhibit 2.2 **Competitive Advantages - The Antidote to Competition**

As already indicated in the previous chapter and as you will read later in more detail, there are actually two separate areas on the whole capitalistic playing field where competitive advantages for the incumbent firm towards the other economic forces can arise.

The first area comprises the relation of a firm towards already existing rivals in the industry, potential rivals, and, last but not least, substitutes. "Indirect" competitive advantages serve in this regard as barriers to entry towards these opponents. Barriers to entry lower competitive pressure for the incumbent firm by holding the adversaries at a distance, keeping them away from taking a hand in the incumbent firm's business matters with its customers and suppliers.

The second area encompasses just the value chain of the business and all direct players on that chain, namely the customers, the incumbent firm itself, and the suppliers. Such "direct" competitive advantages help to bring the incumbent firm into a dominant position to negotiate favourable prices and terms with its customers on the one hand and its suppliers on the other hand.

Crucial to understand for you as investor: all competitive advantages and the resulting dominance strictly stem from two fundamental things – the structural circumstances applying in an industry and a distinct strategy followed by management. Depending on a given industry environment, it is only the degree of management impact that can alter a firm's performance relative to the average peers or comparable industries over time.

Structural circumstances as well as management's plans / actions are inherent in all three layers of a wonderful business. Consequently, the concepts of industry environment and strategy can explain not only strong customer demands and the quality of a good business model but also the secret sauce of predominance in the capitalistic game: competitive advantages.

And although **industry environment** and **strategy** in reality always appear in a kind of blend, understanding the two concepts separately from each other will guide you in the future to better see and evaluate them when looking at companies and industries.

Industry Environment

An industry and its economics evolve from structural circumstances or factors, with the customer at the core. It is the fundamental structure of an industry, an externally given setting from a company's management perspective, that determines the needs / demands, the overall capabilities, the degrees of information, the level of organisation, the number of single participants, the degrees of freedom, the financial power, and ultimately, the magnitude of ascendancy (i.e., negotiation power) of each economic force on the competitive ground. Following that, the allocation of the competitive advantages is given structurally to a large extent, empowering each of the capitalistic players to grab a respective piece of the action.[11]

So in stark contrast to common belief, the firm's management is quite often neither the direct nor the major reason for the financial performance of a company, whatever the performance might be. And as the fundamental structure applies to all incumbent firms within one industry broadly to the same extent, it is not surprising that most of them often have very similar levels of profitability and prospects.

Structural factors substantially demarcate the industry's underlying economics and, with that, the ROIC to be earned on average by the incumbent firms.[12]

But what are now the distinct factors underneath that create and determine the industry environment and, thereby, the basic competitive position and related profit of each economic player?

In principle, the elementary factors that compose an industry environment can be subdivided into three

---

[11] Robert E. Hoskisson, Michael A. Hitt, and R. Duane Ireland, *Competing for Advantage* (Mason, Ohio: Thomson South-Western, 2004).

[12] Pat Dorsey, *The Little Book that Builds Wealth: The Knockout Formula for Finding Great Investments* (Hoboken, New Jersey: John Wiley & Sons, 2008).

categories: first, the human beings and the society with their (customer) needs / demands as the nucleus of each economic system or market; second, technology, physical resources, and the laws of nature as the enabler; third, governmental institutions and macro-economic factors as the frame. All three categories have their own dynamics and aspects but also strongly influence each other.

Human beings and societies have needs and develop demands around which industries emerge; they are the fundamental reason for every market.

True, often the supply side gives the ignition spark by offering some new or changed customer value. Customers try and find out then if they have use for things that have not existed before at all or in that particular form. According to this argumentation, the supply side might be the creator of a market.

But it is still the customers who decide in the following via their buying decisions if the market for a new product or service is viable or not. Therefore, in the long run, it is ultimately the customers on the demand side who are forming a market or industry.

Abraham Maslow conducted studies about healthy, successful, and happy people. He discovered that individuals' needs or motivations have a kind of systematic and universal orderliness. Because of this, all these needs or motivations together can be thought of as being structured in a hierarchy like levels of a pyramid. Once one lower level is achieved, a human being wants to get to the next. Only if the needs of the lower levels are satisfied to a good extent is a human being going for the next higher level. Or the other way around – the next rung of the motivation ladder is only climbed if the individual is not feeling any deficits anymore in his or her current living status.

Maslow's works underline the systematic, fixed order of human desires and impetus, which seems to apply more or less independent from individuals' age, sex, culture, education, social background, religion, or the political system in which people may live. **Maslow's hierarchy of needs** is an acknowledged theory of today's psychology and can help companies as well as investors to comprehend the typical human behaviour with regard to the frequency and urgency of their actual demands and the related buying decisions.

In order to satisfy a customer need and the respective customer demand, a firm has to offer a value proposition via a related business model. Available technology, physical resources, and the laws of nature commonly enable a certain value proposition as well as the respective business model and drive the value creation processes for the customers in all industries. In addition to that, these factors can be the ultimate source of structural competitive advantages in the capitalistic game.

The Internet is a very impressive example of how a ground-breaking technology can not only facilitate new industries but also radically reshape existing industries and competitive settings. With the introduction of that innovation, the World Wide Web, many existing brick-and-mortar retailers were suddenly facing new rivals, which were settling not right across the street but in remote whereabouts, nevertheless being well in touch with the customers via the computer. These new rivals had an attractive offering package, a much lower cost structure, and a high-speed communication line to their customers, putting enormous pressure on traditional incumbents' capital return margins. On top, customers were now able to compare all market offers in seconds in order to pick the greatest deal. This aspect loaded further burden on the old-established incumbents, which had to answer with enriched offerings and revised terms, more efficiency, and finally, their own web presence.

All in all, the customers as one economic party benefited the most from the Internet as a game-changing innovation. Lower prices, better service, and more choice for all the retail customers have been the result of competition at work in the retailing industry since the introduction of the Internet.

Also in the real world, technology, physical resources, and the laws of nature enable businesses and industries on the one hand and systematically drive competition on the other hand.

Machines, working capital, land, skilled people, and technical know-how – for most physical products, these factors are required as input. If a firm requires a large machine outfit so as to generate its customer value, the resulting high fixed costs, mainly in the form of depreciation and amortization, have to be spread over a sales base as large as possible in order to maximise profitability. But because the existing rivals often follow the same logic, the essential need for a big fixed-asset base naturally results in fierce competition in the form of predatory pricing.

The same goes for firms and industries that run highly specialised equipment. Having no alternative use for such tangibles, a firm can't only sell its property and leave the business if capital margins are not sufficient anymore; it would suffer a mammoth loss from the write-off of the assets' values. As a result, such industries have high barriers to leave by nature, which in turn also intensifies the structural pressure on the existing rivals.

Naturally given circumstances like an advantageous location or physical resources with superior qualities can be part of the customer value creation process and, at the same time, can be the sources of competitive advantages. A firm can build stable barriers to entry towards its rivals based on such factors; you will read more about that in the next chapter.

The governmental institutions and macro-economic factors function as the frame in any industry.

Formal laws, regulations, and procedures as well as informal conventions, customs, and norms shape the general socioeconomic activity and the business conduct of the market participants. Set in charge by the government, institutions provide all market participants with the context in which capitalism can work for the best possible outcome.[13] The influence from government and politics can be huge. Laws and regulations as well as subsidies, quotas, minimum wages, taxes, and public bidding procedures can all have a decisive impact on individual industries and the prevailing competitive situation.

Apart from that and as a rule, currencies and interest rates are externally given economic elements

---

[13] Raghuram G. Rajan and Luigi Zingales, *Saving Capitalism from the Capitalists: Unleashing the Power of Financial Markets to Create Wealth and Spread Opportunity* (New Jersey: Princeton University Press, 2004).

that structurally frame industries and permanently influence the competition within.

The nucleus, the enabler, and the frame – each industry is made from these three structural categories. And based on the resulting competitive field, the economic players engage in the capitalistic game.

Keep in mind that the industry environment is dynamic, not static. Following that, the competitive field is also dynamic, not static.[14] Over time, customer needs and relating demands can shift. Consequently, the related industry changes and hence the structural allocation of dominance and negotiation power will alter. Pioneering technology, as described, can structurally change industries and, with that, the competitive setting. And also the governmental setting or certain macro-economic factors can structurally develop over time.

As an investor, you should be cognisant of all these circumstances and see from what angle the changes can come. Some structural factors, like technology, rough up the capitalistic game on a regular basis; others, like the laws of nature, will likely continually remain the same.

There is no clear rule or distinct technique in my view about how to estimate the development of the structural factors and the competitive field; the investor must come to a very individual assessment of the matter.

---

[14] Joan Magretta, *Understanding Michael Porter: The Essential Guide to Competition and Strategy* (Boston: Harvard Business Review Press, 2012).

Strategy

Understood as a management concept, strategy is all about delivering a certain customer value in the best way possible on the one hand and answering to the surrounding industry environment as well as the related competitive situation on the other hand.

So the fact that industry environment gives the ground and frame for every market does not mean that there is no need for management action at all; the industry environment is the basis on which management needs to define its strategy.

Strategy means that a firm's management is deliberately choosing a set of activities to create an, in the optimum, unique customer value compared to its rivals, to excellently run its operations, and, last but not least, to spot and build up a superior position in the capitalistic game.[15] Strategy encompasses all measures a firm's leadership can actively organise in order to be continuously triumphant in a market.

In essence, strategy is a complex composition of planned and executed actions in order to maximise the firm's predominance and profitability while keeping the overall risks at acceptable levels.

And because the industry environment and the corresponding competitive field are dynamic by nature, strategy is a dynamic, never-ending process too.

---

[15] Joan Magretta, *Understanding Michael Porter: The Essential Guide to Competition and Strategy* (Boston: Harvard Business Review Press, 2012).

The strategy process, owned by top management, has to fulfil on principle three paramount tasks:[16]

1. Know the customers' needs / demands
2. Know the company
3. Know the competitive field

All three aspects of **strategic management** - the customers, the company itself, and the general competitive situation - undergo changes and influence each other all the time. Therefore, the management is asked to take an iterative approach. The necessity for action or reaction often changes over time, asking the management to constantly keep an overview and do the right things at the right time. All three aspects must be analysed and considered by the company's management regarding their current state and likely development in the future.

This fundamental analysis must be carried out by the management at any time (e.g., when a firm plans to enter a business, thinks about prime positioning on an existing playing field, or has to consider the withdrawal from a market).

The ultimate goal of strategy is the maximisation of profitability by optimising the position of the firm in the external perspective as well as by perfecting the operating processes in the internal perspective.

In the end, it is about achieving an exceptional ROIC in a market. With that, strategy delivers the explanation for the firm's relative performance compared to its immediate rivals as peers; a good

---

[16] Jack Welch and Suzy Welch, *Winning* (New York: Harper, 2005).

strategy is the reason for a firm's superior performance as measured by the industry's average.

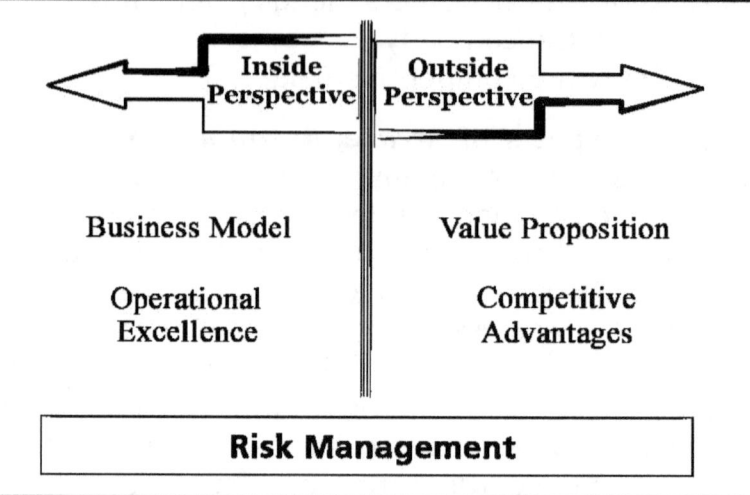

Exhibit 2.3 **Perspectives and Elements of Strategy**

In the outside perspective of strategy, the company's management at first is asked to come up with a distinct, ideally unique value proposition. A company needs to offer a clear-cut value to a chosen set of customers at the right relative price.[17]

It is worthwhile to stress once more that management can't create markets by itself; the customer need is out there in any case. Only the particular way a certain customer value is provided gets designed by management and is put into practice via a respective strategy and related operating processes. Management can discover new customer demands and exploit them by entering that business, maybe even in a unique way. But in any case,

---

[17] Joan Magretta, *Understanding Michael Porter: The Essential Guide to Competition and Strategy* (Boston: Harvard Business Review Press, 2012).

management can't create the customer need and related demand by itself in the long run.

Iteratively and also in this early phase, management has to check whether the firm's internal capabilities are sufficient or can be adjusted in order to create the defined customer value (i.e., satisfy the identified customer demand).

Furthermore, management has to get clear about what it is explicitly not going to do. Only with this additional decision will the firm be able to focus on its chosen mission and vision in the most efficient or productive manner.[18] No less important, chosen trade-offs make the whole idea more distinct and thus harder for others to copy.

At the same time, management must think right from the start about the competitive pressure and adequate means to mitigate this. Management has to go in two directions in this regard. The first way is to identify the competitive forces that create the highest pressure and to find strategic measures against that. By doing so, management actively weakens the competitive advantage from another economic party. The other way a firm's management has to go in parallel is to identify and grow its own strengths by building or occupying competitive advantages on the business landscape.

So before entering a new business, a firm's management needs to identify a market that is or can be protected effectively towards rivals and

---

[18] A *mission* is the stated overall value proposition or business purpose of the company. A *vision* is a (quantitative) long-term goal that describes the ideal, future state of the company. It functions as a North Star for all employees and provides guidance and inspiration for the organisation as a whole.

substitutes. On top, the same management must find the ideal place on the value chain where it has the highest possible negotiation power towards its customers and suppliers, consequently having the ability to take home nice and constant profits.

The value proposition and the planned actions to battle competition together represent the outside perspective of a firm's strategy. You as an investor should try to follow and agree to the management's plans just by applying logic, life experience, and knowledge about economic basics. This exercise is not as hard as commonly thought; the concept of strategy is not as sophisticated as some managers want to suggest.

In the inside perspective of a firm's strategy, then, management is challenged to translate its strategic blueprint into a tailored value chain / a business model (i.e., a set of operating processes inside the organisation). A **business** or **operating process** can be defined as a sequence of interdependent and linked activities that, at every stage, consume and convert resources (e.g., labour, energy, machines, technology) into predefined outputs and finally, customer value. For all intents and purposes, the management is obliged to come up with the best possible outcome regarding the firm's internal capabilities.

In principle, the respective firm should strive to deliver the chosen value proposition different from the activities performed by rivals, lowering the competitive pressure from rivals right from the beginning. All chosen activities should enhance each other by being connected or interwoven in a logical way, aiming all at the same strategic goals. Such strategic fit, along and across the value chain, not only strengthens the firm's value chain as a whole but also makes it even harder for rivals to duplicate the firm's strategy. The management's focus must be on the operating processes that are the most important to create the customer value and that put the potential competitive advantages up. Once defined and prioritised, these **key processes** or **core competencies** ask, of course, for special attention from top management. In some instances, management needs to take decisions and actions just regularly once in a while, sometimes literally every day.

The last thing a good strategy calls for is stability over time. This does not mean that the company should ever stop to optimise all operating processes and the respective network. But keeping the midpoint of the strategy unchanged and consistent gives an organisation time to learn and to become perfect in what it is actually doing.[19]

Once the outside strategy is fine and the relating internal process landscape is set up as described in order to deliver the customer value, good strategy and management are all about running the business in an efficient / productive, safe, reliable, and (environmentally) sustainable way. Striving for such **operational excellence** is a strategic imperative every day and the centrepiece for every thriving company.

Generally, in absence of any potential for

---

[19] Joan Magretta, *Understanding Michael Porter: The Essential Guide to Competition and Strategy* (Boston: Harvard Business Review Press, 2012).

competitive advantages in the external perspective, the internal perspective and the way of realising the value proposition is all the company has to focus on. It actually becomes the only source of economic well-being for the firm.[20] But even if a company is in a very favourable position on the economic playing field, which makes profit creation comparatively easy, operational excellence is a strict must. Being responsible for the shareholders' capital, the management must always try to deliver its value to the customers in the most excellent way possible.

Putting (cost) efficiency and productivity on the front burner helps management to economise money and to enhance output levels. As a direct effect, the overall input-to-output relation of a firm improves. With that, operational excellence has a material impact on the firm's economic performance and hence on its ROIC.

Balanced Scorecard, Kaizen, and Six Sigma are some of the concepts and tools that can help the management to measure and to drive the continuous improvement of the firm's operations. Techniques like benchmarking and related best-in-class-practice sharing, reengineering, quality circles, total quality management, or just-in-time production might be further examples of how management can actively and relentlessly bring operational excellence to higher levels every day.

But operational excellence should not be solely understood as a stubborn mission to minimise costs

---

[20] Pat Dorsey, *The Little Book that Builds Wealth: The Knockout Formula for Finding Great Investments* (Hoboken, New Jersey: John Wiley & Sons, 2008).

or maximise output while striving for highest efficiency or productivity realisable. Efficiency and productivity clearly represent an inherent part of the concept, but translating operational excellence just with these two words would be way too short.

Operational excellence, in my opinion, represents a management philosophy on its own, taking all stakeholders (i.e., shareholders, employees, nature, and society) into account. As an umbrella term, operational excellence encompasses the already mentioned dimensions of safety, reliability, and sustainability too.

The best aspect about operational excellence is that all dimensions can strengthen each other, although you might spontaneously object that safety, reliability, and sustainability do cost money and can slow down processes (i.e., reduce efficiency and productivity).

In sharp contrast to that common belief, I am convinced that the exact opposite is true - at least in the long run. The installation and running of safe, reliable, and sustainable processes might cost real money. But more than money, it requires clear thoughts and the right mind-set in the whole company, lived and empowered by the top management. Once the whole organisation is dedicated to the goal of operational excellence in all its dimensions, operating processes start to run more smoothly and productively over time as learning curve effects kick in. When the organisation is fully up and running, not only does output per time period increase, but input-to-output relations improve as money costs related to downtimes, accidents (measured, e.g., via man-hours lost, lost production time, or compensations to be paid) and pollution (measured, for example, via obligatory and costly cleaning works or law suits) decrease.

Consequently, a company does not only directly benefit from safety, reliability, and sustainability via fewer cash costs, lower operational risks, and higher output per period but also indirectly benefits via more stability in the whole value creation process, with compelling effects on the final product or service quality.

And it gets even better – operational excellence creates value for the customers as well. For instance, the reliable delivery of a product or service can constitute for itself a value for the customer if that customer vitally counts on the quality of the providing firm's input. So if safety, reliability, and sustainability of operations also represent explicit values for the customers, the firm can straightforwardly pass through (i.e., invoice) the costs and time spent to some extent. With that, also the net value for the firm from operational excellence further swells.

Safety, reliability, and sustainability do not cost money but pay off in the total perspective – higher profitability at lower risks. In other words, if cleverly done, investments in operational excellence pay for themselves. At the end, all it takes is a pragmatic management approach, embedded in the overall company's strategy.

In the optimum, operational excellence as a distinct, multi-dimensional management concept can even provide competitive advantages for the respective firm. Striving for operational excellence in all its dimensions can result in permanent cost advantages compared to rivals and substitutes, enhancing the barriers for entry and, therefore, the negotiation power of the incumbent firm on the competitive field.

Apart from that, the preference of today's customer tilts more and more to safe, reliable and sustainable products or services. These days, industry customers face increasing political risks (i.e., reputation risks) if the products or services used in their overall value creation process constantly endanger the health and life of people or the sound condition of the environment. More and more end consumers prefer fair products or services, meaning that price is not the all-dominant purchase criterion anymore – there is also the thoughtful and responsible use of labour force and natural resources during the overall value creation process. So if the buying decision is also influenced by the elements of safety, reliability, and sustainability, operational excellence can establish customer loyalty, which in turn enhances the negotiation power of the incumbent firm, this time directly towards its customers.

As a matter of course, a superior company strives for perfection in its operations; the improving and stabilising effects from all dimensions of operational excellence can upgrade its ROIC to higher quality levels.

Because I believe in the power of operational excellence and its strategic weight for a company's profitability and risk profile, I suggest to hunt only for companies that put all dimensions of this management philosophy on top of their agenda – it will pay off for you as an investor over the years.

The last important question with regard to strategy: how do you spot **good managers** at work? Well, to start with, you should review the firm's overall strategy on the basis of the aspects of a good strategy as described above. In order to corroborate and complement this, I always look for four distinct points.

First: passion and entrepreneurial spirit. Is the management team enthusiastic and serious about its business? Did it, in the best case, found and build the business by itself? Does it hold a considerable equity stake in the undertaking? Only such a management will reliably know and foresee the customers' needs and demands; only such a management will resolutely drive the company in the right direction with a long-term vision.

Second: proven skills in operational excellence. For instance, have the top executives shown in some way that they know how to get the best out of the firm's internal capabilities? How is the firm doing compared to its direct peers in terms of efficiency and productivity? Has the chief management in charge demonstrated that it can put things into action in a timely manner? How is the track record of the company in terms of accidents, hold-ups, and other operational issues? Have the company's managers incorporated the aspect of sustainability with all its facets into the overall process landscape?

Third: wise allocation of capital. Does the firm's highest management understand the competitive advantages of its business and primarily invest in order to sow, build, or strengthen them? Once you have identified the relevant competitive advantages for a company, you will be able to challenge the respective management if it actually knows its own business.

Fourth: candour and humility. Here, you should not only listen to the talk but watch out for the walk. Good managers should practise what they preach. You can't figure this crucial element of good management out from one occurrence but over time, an honest and humble character finds its expression in actions. Just by observing these credible signs, you will find out if the management is as honourable as it claims to be. Does the topmost hierarchy level of a venture earn way more money than any peer in its industry for no understandable reason? Is the management's remuneration totally uncorrelated to the firm's financial performance? Is the compensation of the leadership in a massive disproportion relative to the average employee's salary at the firm? Has an economically well-being management never made any noteworthy charitable donation out of its private pockets? Needless to say, these are not signs that go well together with my picture of a decent, socially minded management.

The Capitalistic Game

III. Economic Moats towards Intruders

Keeping Rivals and Substitutes out of the Game

The dynamics of capitalism guarantee that rivals as well as substitutes – or, in short, intruders - will repeatedly assault any business castle that is earning high capital returns. A genuinely wonderful business must therefore have enduring moats that reliably protect its excellent ROIC. By reducing the competitive pressure from "the outside", economic moats help the incumbent firm to have a constant and above-average income for a long time.

Economic moats make it hard for the intruders to enter and to interfere with the business of the incumbent firm and its customers. With that, economic moats create (additional) relative scarcity of the products or services, which finally results in enhanced negotiation power of the incumbent firm towards its customers. And due to the firm's exclusive position directly on the total value chain, its negotiation power also rises towards its suppliers.

Economic moats can generally be built via **differentiation** of the firm's value proposition and the related business model in two ways – either by a different cost structure or by innovative, legally protected products and services. With that, being an inherent part of every good business strategy, differentiation in essence aims either more on the operating cost structure and the required investments or more on prices, sales units, and the related revenue streams.[21]

To begin with the latter, economic moats can be built from advanced or completely new, effectively unique products or services in the customers' eyes. In such cases, intruders have fundamental difficulties in catching up with their own value propositions to satisfy the customers' demand at all or at the same superiority level. If a value-adding, ground-breaking innovation gets in addition legal protection from the government, the respective creative company can work out an empty market field, enjoying heightened pricing power and profitability. Besides that, economic moats can stem from a superior cost structure relative to the external rivalry too. A flatter or more flexible cost structure can give a company a lasting cost advantage with a positive effect on its ROIC. The rivals or substitutes will constantly operate under pressure, being less profitable or even in the red, when competing with that firm for the same customers.

Both ways, either via a lower cost structure or via innovative, legally protected products and services, a company can get into a predominant position towards

---

[21] Please clearly note that the differentiation has to be an impossible act to follow for the intruders in order to be intrinsically valuable for a company as well as its investors. In other words, differentiation which can be easily imitated by the intruders is meaningless from a valuation standpoint. Truly value-adding differentiation always establishes an insurmountable economic moat as a protective shield against intruders. Ergo, it is not only necessary to meet a particular customer demand in a differentiated (i.e., more cost efficient and / or significantly improved) way; the company must also be capable of locking its peers and substitutes out somehow so that nobody spoils the moneymaking party.

its rivals and substitutes. The resulting economic moats keep such external rivalry away from (easily) doing business with the customers and suppliers, while the fortunate company experiences an elevated profitability within the boundaries of its stronghold.

Important also from an investor's standpoint - some differentiation strategies perform better than others because some resulting economic moats are more durable and wider by nature. Economic moats resting on structural circumstances of the industry environment are in principle more durable and wider than barriers to entry that are purely "man-made" or only based on a management plan; advantages from tangible assets and physical settings are normally just harder to copy than intangibles like thoughts and theoretical concepts. In the case of a structural advantage from the industry environment, the first mover often irreversibly occupies the respective position, which can't be easily, or at all, overcome by the intruders.

Due to this reason, once you have spotted an "indirect" competitive advantage that is working, you first need to get a solid idea about its source; then, you have to estimate its durability and width. In order to understand and estimate the quality of a barrier to entry from an investor's perspective, the leading questions are: "What does it take to establish a viable position in that particular industry? How could I theoretically do business with the customer instead of the incumbent firm on a sustainable basis?" In more technical terms, you would ask yourself for the reproduction costs of the business, explicitly including the costs to overcome (i.e., replicate) the economic moats of the industry or firm under scrutiny.

Innovative, Legally Protected Products or Services

Creativity is one big engine for every economy's development. Igniting ideas are valuable for the whole society as newly invented products and services can be of immense use for many individuals. Regrettably, good ideas are pretty quickly copied and sold for cheap by people who want to ride the wave for free. But as innovative ideas have generally such a positive impact on society, the government normally wants to foster and shelter ingenuity. Therefore, in order to incentivise the inventive individuals or companies on the one hand and to inhibit plagiarism on the other hand, intellectual property can get legal protection via a **patent**.[22]

A patent helps a pioneering company to get rewarded for its creativity as well as its financial investments made in the new products or services. Due to the patent, the new product or service can't be copied or easily substituted anymore. After the company's management and employees have worked hard to get the advanced product or service into the marketplace, the patent works as a structural shield towards external rivalry. Under the protective umbrella of a patent, the respective firm enjoys unsaturated markets (i.e., a kind of legal monopoly)

---

[22] A patent might be granted for any new and useful item, process, or composition of matter or for any new and useful improvement thereof. But more than that, the underlying invention must also be novel too. That means that a patentable invention should neither have existed before nor be an obvious improvement or alteration of a previously known invention.

with virtually no competition from external rivalry, high growth, and rich capital return margins.

This is what patents generally do, but while they can result in tremendously valuable economic moats, they are not always as steadfast as you might think.

To start with, patents have a finite life, and it is a virtual certainty that copyists will arrive as soon as a profitable patent expires. In the pharmaceutical industry, this fact drives a whole industry of its own that produces generic medications once the effective originals lose their protection from patents. Legal manoeuvring can sometimes extend the life of a patented product or service, but guessing which team of lawyers will win a patent battle is a game with poor odds – unless you manage to specialise in intellectual property law, of course.

Furthermore, patents are not irrevocable either; they can be challenged even during their lifetime, and the more profitable the patent is, the more lawyers will try to come up with ways to attack it. Many generic drug firms, to pick up the example again, make challenging the big pharmaceutical companies' patents a prominent part of their business. They may succeed with only one trial in ten, but the payoff for a single fruitful attempt is so high that the charges keep coming.

Therefore, please stay clear of any firm that relies only on one patented product or service for its profits, as any challenge to this patent can severely harm the company. Apart from this, please be wary of innovative companies that promise future returns from a single patent sounding too good to be true –

oftentimes, that is exactly what these returns turn out to be.

The only time patents constitute a veritably enduring economic moat is when the firm and its management have demonstrated a track record of innovation that is very likely to continue, as well as a wide variety of patented products or services.

Only that way an investor can ascertain if the underlying research and development (R&D) process works or not. Think of large pharmaceutical conglomerates such as Novartis or Pfizer, which have literally thousands of patents on hundreds of different product types and treatments. These firms have been cranking out patents for years, and their historical success gives reasonable assurance that currently patented products will likely be replaced by new ones to come.

Let's take DuPont as another palpable example. DuPont's vision has always been to apply world-class science to enable a better, safer, and healthier life for people everywhere. Having an extraordinary range of materials science, chemistry, biological science, and engineering capabilities in-house, the firm offers a broad choice of innovative, sustainable, and highly demanded products to all kind of industry customers. Aiming at substantial global trends and needs, its strategic focus thereby lies in three market areas: agriculture and nutrition, bio-based industrials, and advanced materials.

To unleash the full-blown power of its internal R&D capabilities and to get the reward from the market for its achieved innovations, DuPont developed a unique invention delivery system. Think of it like a bridge –

from laboratory to market. On the one side is the customer need, on the other side, the science and engineering competences. DuPont connects its global market insights, exceptional science, and honed technical skills to lay a seamless path from need to market. This integrated system enables the company to swiftly develop cutting-edge products and to bring superior products to the customers faster and more effectively than other firms. In the whole invention delivery system, the R&D process, with its nearly ten thousand scientists and engineers at more than 150 R&D centres and thirteen innovation hubs around the globe, builds the backbone of DuPont's competitive advantage from innovative technology.

Rooted in science, driven by engineering, DuPont is first-class when it comes to turning scientific breakthroughs into commercial breakouts. All of its business streams call upon DuPont's world-class science and technology, deep understanding of commercial value chains, and technical knowledge to deliver value-added, proprietary solutions.

That not only sets DuPont apart from many rivals in its field but also puts high value growth opportunities up, which can then be tapped by DuPont as the unchallenged first mover.

But it is not only highly sophisticated industries like pharmaceutical or special chemistry where an investor can find companies which outstand with a technological leadership strategy. Also in the food and beverage industry, novel technology can be a driver for new revenues and a source of an economic moat.

For PepsiCo, to give a fitting example, fresh technology is one strategic pillar as well as one source for competitive advantages.

Customers' tastes change, and people like to try something new from time to time. Apart from that, basic human requirements such as nutrition can undergo fundamental changes too. The people in this day and age put more and more emphasis on the quality of the foods and drinks they consume. Eating and drinking are not only about satisfying the urgent needs from hunger and thirst anymore but are things to be enjoyed in good company with mindfulness. People start to ask for transparency along the total value chain and sustainable production measures. A responsible use of human labour as well as environmental resources has become a bigger part of the final consumers' buying decision.

To meet those evolving needs and resulting demands, PepsiCo constantly must adapt, advance, and innovate. Therefore, PepsiCo's R&D function closely works with its business partners in order to deliver on today's brand and market priorities as well as to set up the growth opportunities of tomorrow.

Here again, the prime focus is on the resulting customers' demand. Based on that, the value proposition is set and adjusted, if necessary. The R&D team encompasses experts with traditional food and beverage science skills as well as experts from newer scientific areas such as agronomy, exercise physiology, metabolomics, rheology, and computational nutrition analysis. A R&D function that for decades was focused almost exclusively on the consumers' taste experience began at some point in time to bring the consumers' overall biology into the picture. To deliver the right product offerings, all preference drivers such as taste, aroma, texture, content, environmental footprint, and convenience are today analysed and considered in the total value creation process.

The requirement for change is not easy for many food and beverage companies, as the consumers of today are actually asking for the best aspects of two different worlds. On the one hand, consumers want more nutritious products with reduced levels of sodium, saturated fats, and added sugars. In addition, the production methods must meet higher ethical and environmental standards. On the other hand, consumers still expect PepsiCo's portfolio to deliver the same taste experience. In other words, customers today ask for a significantly mutated value proposition compared to the past.

Hence, PepsiCo must not only come up with new recipes, packing units, or package designs. Innovation is a key process that affects all processes along the entire value chain, including purchasing, production, and distribution.

For example, new production technologies were needed to remove literally thousands of metric tons of sodium from the total product portfolio in central global markets. By switching in certain instances to oils that contain less saturated fats and by providing more snacks that are baked rather than fried, PepsiCo has achieved significant reductions in saturated fats.[23]

PepsiCo's current product portfolio would not be the same without innovation. Actually, the portfolio of today is a direct result of PepsiCo's constant, never-ending R&D process. Innovation and technology are the way to adapt to an altering environment and

---

[23] See Newfoodmagazine, PepsiCo, Issue 4 / 2015.

related shifts in the customers' needs and demands. Only the companies that quickly find their feet in a new situation have a chance to survive and prosper; the others, which are not able to do so, will lose ground.

On top of this, the R&D process allows PepsiCo to create additional growth by exploiting fresh trends as the first mover. High-tech soda dispensers, for example, offer end consumers a broad choice of beverages that goes far beyond the former options with the older machines. Apart from that, people just enjoy the modern design and active handling of the novel dispensers. PepsiCo's immediate customers, namely the grocery shops, convenience stores, and other retail outlets, experience more soda sales and overall consumer traffic. So all parties benefit from PepsiCo's richness of ideas.

As you can see, leading-edge technology drives a company's success in two major ways - adaptation of changes in customer demand and creation of (new) growth. By enabling faster adjustment of the value proposition to changing trends and (unchallenged) growth, R&D is one of PepsiCo's key processes to ensure its superior position relative to many rivals and to propel the long-term success of this outstanding company.

The cocoa and chocolate manufacturer Barry Callebaut is definitely another inventive company within the food and beverage sector worth mentioning here. Although its business is predominantly about volume and cost leadership, another pillar of Barry Callebaut's overall business strategy is actually science and technology.

In its global innovation centres in Wieze, Belgium, for chocolate and Louviers, France, for cocoa, the group focuses on developing unique capabilities and expertise in fields of innovation like "cocoa science". With over ten thousand bioactive components, cocoa is one of the most complex food products. Through fundamental research into the secrets of the cocoa bean, Barry Callebaut has been able to deliver insights that address current customer trends and business needs. In the field of research "reformulation of chocolate and cocoa products", the company constantly tries to come up with novel products and applications that offer a better energy balance and an improved product composition, without compromising on taste and perceived indulgence. In another field of research, the company works on the perfection of chocolate's fundamental attributes, namely structure, texture, and sensory perception.

All these efforts in technology taken together give the Swiss cocoa and chocolate giant the potential to enrich / enlarge its value proposition in general, to differentiate its sweet products clearly from rivals in the customers' opinions, and, last but not least, to tap into new and unchallenged markets.

And although new recipes, bottle designs, or other innovative ideas in the food and beverage industry often do not qualify for a patent, they surely can be protected from plagiarism via **trade secrets**, **trademarks**, or **copyrights**. Once erected by management, these measures also constitute valuable assets for the possessing firm as they create structural moats towards external rivalry.

In a nutshell, new technology can work as a barrier to entry for intruders under two equally important preconditions.

First, the company has really incorporated innovation into its business model via a functioning, value-creating R&D process. You should not look for a one-trick pony but for companies that have a proven track record and a broad pipeline of innovative products or services – hence, modern ways to satisfy evolving customer demands.

Second, the novelty a firm has come up with should possess institutional protection in the form of patents or the like. Only that way can you be reasonably sure that the creative company gets structural shelter from its external rivalry and can, at least for a while, exclusively pocket the well-deserved reward for all the endured troubles as well as the taken risks. On top, you should find out how the expiration schedule of the firm's patent portfolio looks like and how secure the intellectual property in the relevant markets generally is.

Cost Advantages

Obviously, cost advantages matter most in industries where innovation and related technology can't add too much value anymore to the central products or services. In such industries, products or services are perceived as a kind of commodity by the customers where the respective prices (i.e., costs) become the major aspect in the customers' purchase decision process. For this reason, the cost structure (i.e., the operating costs as well as the capital investment needs) represents the only true differentiator for the competing firm towards its peers and substitutes.

Cost advantages and related economic moats can, by and large, stem from the following sources:

1. Size / Economies of scale
2. Synergies / Economies of scope
3. Superior process management
4. Advantageous locations
5. Niche markets / Efficient scale effect
6. Closer distance and higher (local) density
7. Unique natural resources
8. Better application and compliance processes

As already stated earlier, whether a cost advantage actually puts up a meaningful and durable economic moat for the respective firm depends on how easily the source for the cost advantage can be replicated by others. By asking yourself this question, you will find out, solely by applying logic, if you are eyeing a lasting competitive advantage from a cost perspective or not.

1. Size / Economies of Scale

There are actually many examples of economically well-being companies that are at the same time the biggest in their industry with regard to revenues. Size seems to be a sign of financial success, but it is not necessarily the original source of it. To tell you the truth right away, economies of scale do not always function as a competitive advantage for an incumbent firm because they do not always reliably serve as barriers to entry towards rivals and substitutes.

To understand competitive advantages from economies of scale, it is first important to comprehend the term **scale effect**, which stems from the nature of fixed (i.e., indirect) costs. The scale effect just describes that the average costs per unit decrease if fixed costs are spread over an increasing sales base.[24] Subsequently, from a certain **break-even point** onwards, profits accrue and rise more strongly in percentage terms than the ascending sales as only variable (i.e., direct) costs follow them up, while fixed costs stay flat (in a certain range of output).

More importantly, the reason for the fixed costs is irrelevant for the (structural) scale effect. Every company will have some capital investments with pre-set depreciation expenditures in turn and some operating processes that trigger fixed spending; every company will have some bank debts in the balance sheet and an overhead organisation in place in order to run the show, causing cash costs at some static level.

With that, no matter if the fixed costs come from ongoing operations, investments in operational equipment, or just financing activities, literally every company with fixed costs in its total cost structure experiences a scale effect on unit costs, and a **leverage effect** on profitability in turn, if its sales volume rises.[25]

---

[24] Aka *fixed-cost degression*.

[25] The leverage effect on the return on equity (ROE) ratio can generally come from **operational leverage** (i.e., fixed costs in the operating cost structure) as well as **financial leverage** (i.e., fixed interest payments to banks and the like). The ROIC ratio can only be impacted by operational leverage.

As you learn in this book, the true source of many competitive advantages lies in exceptional operating processes and the way management has put them into practice. Purchasing, R&D, business development (i.e., bidding / application) and (legal) compliance, production, marketing and sales, logistics and distribution – each of these operating processes leads to a considerable level of fixed costs but can also be the source of a meaningful and sustainable competitive advantage for a firm. The bigger or more forceful such key processes get, the more economies of scale kick in as a structural element too.

Due to that, businesses that possess competitive advantages from specific operating processes in addition often benefit from the scale effect. Critically here, the scale effect strengthens the original competitive advantage but does not cause it. At the beginning, it takes management action to set up an unparalleled process, and it normally requires considerable time, effort, and money to build it. But once the firm's leadership has put a clear competitive advantage up in one operational area, the scale effect can be of big help in order to fortify and defend it in a structural manner. With that, the size of an undertaking in revenue terms and the related scale effect often structurally underpin the management-made competitive advantage coming from a certain operating process.

But, yes, a sizable top line can also be used as a distinct measure in a firm's business strategy to establish a durable and wide economic moat towards external rivalry. Due to the scale effect, in some industries it is vitally important to seek market leadership, so trying to be the biggest just in revenue terms. The fixed costs get spread over a bigger sales base, providing the largest firm with a relative cost advantage compared to its existing and potential rivals or substitutes as well as a leverage on its profits; this is particularly true in the already mentioned volume and commodity-like businesses.

If a company wants to succeed with a clear size strategy regarding revenues, three preconditions must be met:[26]

- ➢ The fixed costs must be a major part of the natural total cost structure (i.e., total value creation process) within the industry
- ➢ The price is the only / major buying criterion for the customers
- ➢ The company occupies the major part of a clearly defined, relevant market

Meeting these three points, the size in revenues and the related scale effect can work for a firm as an economic moat.

The first point is obvious: fixed costs with their specific nature trigger the scale effect as explained. So to have the scale effect as a possible source of an economic moat, fixed costs have to be a major and inherent part of the total cost structure of a company as well as of the respective industry. For instance, if the industry is very capital-intensive by nature, the most advisable strategy for each firm in order to reach profitability is logically to spread the resulting fixed

---

[26] Bruce Greenwald and Judd Kahn, *Competition Demystified: A Radically Simplified Approach to Business Strategy* (New York: Portfolio, 2007).

costs from depreciation over a sales base that is as large as possible.

The second point stresses that such a purely size-based economic moat works most effectively in markets where the price is the central decision criterion for a customer to purchase; the firm can't differentiate itself in the eyes of the customers by other means than its cost structure and related pricing.

Due to these two first points, economies of scale exist mostly in volume industries with high capital expenditure needs and undifferentiated products or services. Classic examples for capital-intensive volume businesses are beer breweries, steel mills, concrete plants, and telecommunication companies.[27]

At the time of publication, Barry Callebaut is the world's leading manufacturer of high-quality cocoa and chocolate, serving customers in the entire food industry as well as end consumers in many countries directly with a broad product portfolio. Cocoa and chocolate production is fundamentally a capital-intensive volume business, asking in the first place for a concentrated cost leadership strategy. But cost leadership is a relative thing and can be achieved by either growing the top line or by curbing costs. Knowing that, Barry Callebaut puts emphasis not only on operating processes, cost efficiency, and productivity but also on (organic as well as inorganic)

---

[27] Heather Brilliant and Elizabeth Collins, *Why Moats Matter: The Morningstar Approach to Stock Investing* (Hoboken, New Jersey: John Wiley & Sons, 2014).

revenue growth in order to lower the average cost per unit of cocoa or chocolate.

Last but not least, a company needs to be big in a distinctive area – big in relation to the immediate rivals as well as big in relation to the specific marketplace, defined by customer type or product scope, where it wants to exercise its domination power from size in revenues.

Consequently, the strategic goal must generally be to control a relatively substantial share in the so-called **relevant market**.[28] With regard to the economic moat from economies of scale, it is not the total sum of all the firm's revenue streams that matters towards peers. Revenues from the firm's other businesses just do not count, as they do not impact the firm's competitive position in the market in which it is battling for the customer's choice; such size does not allow a sustainably lower cost structure in a particular market and hence does not put concrete cost pressure on direct rivals. In such cases, the rivals with which a company is competing can still breathe as their sales base is sufficiently large, allowing them at least to cover their fixed costs and make a simple living in the relevant market.

Therefore, the definition of the relevant market must be precise and clear-cut. Only then can the dominating company challenge its rivals on the cost

---

[28] Bruce Greenwald and Judd Kahn, *Competition demystified: A Radically Simplified Approach to Business Strategy* (New York: Portfolio, 2007).

side and make its strategic decisions in a proper way.[29]

But relevant markets can also be limited too narrowly by management. Some firms delineate their playing field very rigidly in order to proudly claim to be the market leader in that particular space. Tightening the relevant market definition and the respective range of rivals too much, however, will make the scale strategy ineffective as well. In the worst case, this management mistake can cause a wrong strategic approach with very negative implications for the respective firm.

The primary strategy as a market leader is not to grow but to defend its pole position and relative market dominance, whereas the strategy of the second or third company in the field is, as an iron rule, to close in on the leader by all means. By seeing itself incorrectly as the market leader, a firm would not think in growth terms anymore and would lose further ground in the capitalistic battle. In consequence, such a company gets dethroned in the market it once claimed to be the leader of. In the worst-case scenario, it needs to completely withdraw from that business area as normally only the first two or at most three companies in volume markets can achieve a sustainable profitability in order to exist and prosper.[30]

Bringing it all together, occupying and defending a significant share in a properly defined, relevant

---

[29] Tim Koller, Richard Dobbs, and Bill Huyett, *Value: The Four Cornerstones of Corporate Finance* (Hoboken, New Jersey: John Wiley & Sons, 2011).
[30] Jack Welch and Suzy Welch, *Winning* (New York: Harper, 2005).

market is the strategic imperative for a company that wants to build a barrier to entry from its economies of scale. An economic moat from scale asks management to constantly watch the market and to defend its (dominant) share.

Logically, the benefit from pure size applies mostly for the biggest player (i.e., market leader); that's why it is the most desired position for every firm in this game. In order to shield the pole position and related benefits, the market leader has to occupy so much of the market in terms of revenues that the rest of the market is not big enough for the other rivals to make a proper living. Firms need a certain size in terms of revenues just to cover their fixed costs and to start to make cash profits. In the long term, they would need to cover their capital costs on top, as they would expect a compensation for the risks and challenges taken on in the business; but this is exactly the line of defence for the biggest firm.

Catching up with the market leader in terms of revenues via organic growth, once the market hierarchy is established, is extremely tough. Physically, there might be no barriers for new entrants and the already-chasing peers to conduct business. But (organically) growing revenues in order to catch up with the incumbent market leader is practically near to impossible. This especially holds true if the market as a whole is not growing anymore and additional size can only be realised by taking away revenues from the other incumbent producers or service providers. Too strong are the cost advantages for the biggest firms in such a saturated industry; too strong are the headwinds for the smaller ones from likely price wars. If a smaller player would follow a growth strategy in such a mature market, it would take a long time to gain relative size with huge pressure on profitability. As its profitability is already lower due to a lower sales base, every further cut on price can bring it into existential trouble.

Also the market leader might only appear to be the winner. Putting it frankly, if fights about market share are only conducted via price cuts, there is never a real victor under the battling firms. Not only the smaller players' profitability gets under colossal pressure; the market leader's coffer is hit by the price cuts too. This is the major drawback of this strategy (i.e., competitive advantage), also from an investor's perspective.

Nonetheless, a firm can erect a barrier to entry from pure size measured in revenues that works due to the structural scale effect, leaving smaller rivals with a constant cost disadvantage. If it comes to economies of scale, the strategic imperative number one for the management is to build up the size of the company's top line in the fastest manner possible.

Once the market leadership is established in one relevant market, via organic or inorganic growth, the respective firm's management has to ceaselessly oversee and manage all developments in order to hold its relative dominance.

So this economic moat has also structural as well as strategic elements. Constant (strategic) management attention is mandatory to benefit from the (structural) scale effect over an extended period of time.

2. Synergies / Economies of Scope

Synergies between separate lines of business and related **economies of scope** can represent a strong approach for a firm to create enduring cost advantages compared to its external rivalry.

Economies of scope, just like the economies of scale, describe a structural effect on a company's average cost structure. As a result of increasing the number of different goods produced or services provided by one company, the average costs per sales unit decrease. Other than economies of scale, economies of scope are efficiencies from a wisely combined variety of complementary businesses, not from the magnitude of one single business line.

There are two general ways to lift economies of scope.

First, economies of scope can come from the horizontal bundling of input factors – operational assets, human capacities, processes, technology, location, and time - that amplifies the width of the value creation potential. It just saves costs in total perspective if the same facilities and resources can be used to generate different types of products or services. Also, the production at the same location or at the same time reduces the average conversion costs of a bundle of products or services.

Second, economies of scope can come from a vertical linking of value chains, which increases the depth of the value creation potential. By bringing consecutively linked business lines under one single company's organisational umbrella, the existing facilities and resources can be directly used or easily customised for these additional businesses as well, creating opportunities to eliminate redundancies, to tame operational risks, and to generate cost efficiencies along larger parts of a complete value chain.

Logically, synergies and the corresponding economies of scope are most influential when they are already an inherent part of the company's value proposition and the related business model.

BASF, currently the world's largest chemical company by revenues, controls synergies that have led to lasting cost advantages compared to its peers. The cost advantages BASF possesses compared to its rivals come not just from the company's scale and its technological leadership position but from its unique "Verbund" production process system. Everything in this management approach is about intelligent interlinking of production plants, material flows, and infrastructure in order to maximise efficiency and productivity. Apart from this, know-how and customers are cleverly connected to each other, improving the overall production sequences even further. BASF also uses the term "Verbund" to label its six massive chemical complexes around the globe. To give an idea of the size of these operations, the firm's German site includes around two hundred production plants and employs more than thirty-five thousands people, with a total site area of around ten square kilometres; it is the largest integrated chemical complex in the world.

A Verbund hosts various chemical plants that extend from basic chemicals right through to higher-value-added products such as coatings or crop protection agents. In addition, by-products from one plant can be used as input material at another. The underlying logic extends to energy use as well, where heat from production processes at one plant can be harnessed and used as an alternative power source at a neighbouring plant.

By grouping many different value chains closely together and integrating the production vertically as well as horizontally, the group saves on transportation costs, consumes less energy, and enjoys higher product yields. This leads to huge gains in efficiency and productivity and hence to massive economies of scope.

BASF itself estimates that its Verbund concept saves operating costs in excess of $ 1 billion per annum compared to the rivals' production methods. This is a meaningful amount considering that the earnings before interests and taxes in 2015 were $ 6.9 billion.[31] And although other chemical companies also operate world-class facilities with state-of-the-art technology, very few, if any, match the Verbund concept of sophistically linking numerous plants in concert at one site with the principle that each product can be of use for the others. While waste and time get minimised, efficiency and productivity are brought to their physical limits.[32]

As you see, synergies and related economies of scope can work nicely as economic moats if the various business lines and the overall business model of the company fit to each other. Synergies provide then the

---

[31] Wayne T. Smith, *BASF Roadshow New York & Boston* (Boston: 22nd / 23rd March, 2016).

[32] Heather Brilliant and Elizabeth Collins, *Why Moats Matter: The Morningstar Approach to Stock Investing* (Hoboken, New Jersey: John Wiley & Sons, 2014).

respective company with sustainable cost advantages towards its peers.

But economies of scope have, in contrast to economies of scale, no clear optimum. Furthermore, the maximum benefit from synergies is pretty hard to determine and can also change over time. To benefit from economies of scale, the management simply needs to maximise revenues in the relevant market. But in order to benefit from economies of scope, the management has to find the right balance between synergies on the one hand and complexity as well as inflexibility on the other hand. The economics and corporate cultures of businesses naturally differ very often, which in principle bedevils the combination of different lines of business. Due to that, just adding different business lines and related revenue streams will not do the trick. The wise choice of business areas and the right degree regarding vertical as well as horizontal integration are key, hence requiring business acumen and operational management skills. A sound business understanding helps to detect the right fits; a good process management finally gives reasonable security to achieve the desired synergies by moderating complexity and inflexibility.

Way too often, however, the plan of many companies to realise synergies just by bringing unlike business lines below one management does not work out. Many businesses are already structurally too diverse to have any meaningful synergy potential; some are even as different as chalk and cheese. After such an unsuitable combination, it is then often merely a common IT platform the dissimilar businesses share under the same organisational roof. The frequently given argument to have synergies in the management capabilities does not sound really convincing either, as the thorough management of only one business should be more than a part-time job. As an unwished result, instead of synergies lifted, often even more costs accrue in consequence of the composite company's swollen complexity and increased inflexibility. In such cases, the sum of the parts is logically worth more than the conglomerate as a whole.

From a value perspective, it is then better to untangle the different business areas or to refocus the firm's business model again on the total value chain rather than to keep the inefficient construct alive. Not surprisingly, it is mainly such uneconomical conglomerates that are regularly targeted by activist investors. Just by splitting a misshapen organisational complex into proper parts, such investors create shareholder value, unleashing the power of each business line or transformation phase on the total value chain, ultimately revealing that synergies did not exist in the first place. After the split, each separate business area can concentrate on its specific strengths and weaknesses, develop a more effective strategy on its own, and head in an unhindered manner for more growth and profitability.

Wells Fargo, one of the biggest and most successful banks in the United States, is another good example for benefiting from economies of scope in a smart way.

This bank has grown an impressively profitable business by adopting a strategy that some people would describe as boring; it primarily focusses on the basics of banking – deposits and loans. Around these plain but central themes, which naturally create a long-term relationship with a bank customer, Wells Fargo has built a business model that be run safely with a sound risk management strategy as well as in an efficient and productive way.

Another key to success is Wells Fargo's direct access to individual customers due to its unrivalled branch network. Being in close contact with its customers, face-to-face, the bank with the stagecoach logo can offer various finance products and services around its bread-and-butter business out of one hand, resulting in huge cross-selling opportunities. From checking accounts and debit cards to savings products and treasury management services, Wells Fargo helps an extensive range of customers to manage their daily financial lives.

And as the bank's complete product and service portfolio can be facilitated from one common resource base, all this translates into synergetic cost advantages for Wells Fargo compared to its peers. Resources such as personnel, IT systems, and related data as well as other operational assets can be commonly used in order to provide all kinds of financial services and products.

From a customer's viewpoint, the overall value proposition of Wells Fargo is comprehensive and hence more convenient and compelling compared to the ones of other banks.

By providing strength and stability, its diversified business model allows Wells Fargo to excel when other banks do not; Wells Fargo clearly has a competitive lead due to economies of scope.

3. Superior Process Management

Advantages on the competitive field from a leading process management are fascinating because, in theory, they should not exist for long enough to constitute much of an economic moat. After all, if a company figures out a way to deliver a product or service at lower cost or to offer a better quality for the same price, would not a logical step for its rivals be to quickly copy that blueprint so they can match the leader's operations and cost structure?

Well, this does happen eventually in most instances. But in some cases, it can take much more time and effort than one might expect. And while rivals try to make up leeway, the originator of the superior process system can make a lot of money.[33]

In general, a ceaseless focus on optimisation in all operational matters is a strategic imperative for every company, as the management is responsible for the optimal utilisation of the shareholders' capital. And for companies that have no potential for any kind of competitive advantages, constant improvement of the overall operations is actually the only possibility to stay in the capitalistic game.

Nevertheless, there are in fact some well-managed companies around that have been able to outperform their peers over long periods of time in industries without any potential barriers to entry in place. This is because, in blunt contrast to prevailing

---

[33] Heather Brilliant and Elizabeth Collins, *Why Moats Matter: The Morningstar Approach to Stock Investing* (Hoboken, New Jersey: John Wiley & Sons, 2014). Tim Koller, Richard Dobbs, and Bill Huyett, *Value: The Four Cornerstones of Corporate Finance* (Hoboken, New Jersey: John Wiley & Sons, 2011).

opinions in the economic community, firms are not all equally good at orchestrating available tangible assets, human capabilities, and technologies or exploiting existing data and market opportunities. In reality, there are modifications in management effectiveness and business strategies that can make a huge difference in the relative financial performance between peers - even over the long haul.[34]

In addition, some companies are so good at constantly driving efficiency and productivity or even at operational excellence as the whole management concept that these capabilities constitute on their own a lasting competitive advantage towards rivals.

The management in these companies know their daily businesses and the related value drivers. And they know how to put things into practise due to their superior process management skills. With that, companies can build a sustainable economic moat from superior process management if that topic is put highest on the daily agenda.

A model for superior process management is McDonald's. This globally operating company has literally founded its value proposition and related business model on efficiency / productivity and reliability (i.e., consistency).

Unquestioned, the company is the world's leading fast food service retailer with over thirty-six thousand restaurants in over one hundred countries around the globe. McDonald's built its fast food imperium around consistent, perfect French fries. Fast, cheap, and convenient food - a pretty simple value proposition at

---

[34] Bruce Greenwald and Judd Kahn, *Competition Demystified: A Radically Simplified Approach to Business Strategy* (New York: Portfolio, 2007).

first glance. But do not get me wrong – simple does not mean primitive or dull in this context.

The company just took the term "fast food" pretty seriously, defined a clear-cut value proposition, and designed the process landscape while perpetually taking its key success factors speed, consistency, and costs into consideration. This actually requires a huge strategic effort from management and relentless focus on every detail of the value chain while keeping the overall picture in mind; a superior process landscape calls for a lot of time and brain. This way, McDonald's has been able to gain and hold its market leadership position in the fast food industry over decades. Everything in its well-oiled process system is tailored in order to deliver the value proposition in a speedy, consistent, and cost efficient manner. Optimising processes is not only in the management's daily mind set, but it is in the management's DNA.[35]

Without a doubt, McDonald's also has an immense marketing machine running, but simplicity and focus on best practices are the main ingredients in the recipe for success under the "Golden Arches".

Its management is actually doing the common things, just much better than any other fast food chain. No one in the industry has standardised its range of articles to that extent, no one has dovetailed its supply chains, logistics, and restaurant operations more efficiently. That way, the company has eliminated complexity in its process landscape, which results in higher scalability and a flatter total costs curve compared to peers. Operations also become

---

[35] Joan Magretta, *Understanding Michael Porter: The Essential Guide to Competition and Strategy* (Boston: Harvard Business Review Press, 2012).

safer and more sustainable if done in an organised as well as focussed routine. The result of that is less operational risks for McDonald's, impacting the profitability positively from the cost angle over time.

These main factors together - the simple but compelling value proposition translated into a sound business model, safeguarded by the cost advantages from superior process management, have made McDonald's one of the most profitable and successful companies of the last several decades.[36]

---

[36] McDonald's has enjoyed above-average profitability over a long period of time due to what I would call a good strategy / business model. In the early 1940s, Richard and Maurice McDonald came up with the value proposition to serve food and beverages in the style we still know today. That was kind of unique in those days. Together with Raymond Kroc they started then the restaurant chain model and perfected the mentioned competitive advantage from superior process management that has put them apart from their upcoming peers for decades. McDonald's found a good trade-off about what to do and what not to do. Thereby, it also clearly defined its core customers. All in its value chain is done to maximise speed and consistency, aiming to constantly deliver the value proposition in the most efficient way. With that, the company also absorbed the last criterion for a good strategy, namely consistency over time. But despite this remarkable strategy, the issue for McDonald's in our days is that the average customers' taste (i.e., the customers' need and demand) has changed. People of today put more and more emphasis on healthy quality food, even when it comes to burgers and fries. This new demand requires more time and more complex processes - a straight threat to McDonald's core competencies. How to bring together the standardised and quick menu with the individualisation of the customer demand? How to deliver enhanced quality in an appealing ambience to new customers if the core customers are still primarily looking for an inexpensive and convenient meal? It remains to be seen if McDonald's will be able to react to this structural shift in the customer demand without putting its strategy in jeopardy.

All its efforts in every detail of the operating processes pay off for McDonald's in the form of lasting cost advantages compared to the rivalling fast food chains or other gastronomy concepts.

As the icing on the cake, scale advantages help McDonald's to strengthen its position further in various operational areas like marketing or purchase. And to make the picture complete, McDonald's increasingly benefits from economies of scope by preparing not only burgers and fries but also fast, convenient, and affordable breakfast or coffee specialities and pastries at the same location with the same production facilities.

Apart from outstanding management effort and coordination talent, pioneering technology can effectuate competitive cost advantages from a superior process system too. Optimally, an innovation in the process landscape gets legal protection via a patent or the like.

Coming back to BASF, this company developed, for instance, a new, proprietary acrylic-acid process technology that results in significantly lower production costs compared to the industry average. Efficiency gains from this best-in-class production process stem from run-time extensions, higher throughput, and lower energy consumption.[37]

Logically, it will be the companies persistently seeking operational excellence that will find new areas for process improvement in their operations as the first player. Being an early bird gives such firms at least a

---

[37] Wayne T. Smith, *BASF Roadshow New York & Boston* (Boston: 22nd / 23rd March, 2016).

temporary lead, which is then strengthened by the structural ***experience curve effect***.[38]

Yet an investor should keep in mind that, apart from the structural advantage from the learning curve effect, a superior process landscape is a kind of economic moat which is all "man-made" in principle, asking for management attention literally every day. With that, superior process management skills and organisation talent can result in strong and enduring cost advantages as one kind of economic moat towards external rivalry. But this moat also can be overcome if the underlying knowledge can't be legally protected by a patent or similar means.

Hence, for you as an investor, it is key to identify this kind of economic moat at its early stage in order to benefit from it as long as possible. And you might also want to closely watch the developments. Peers can either copy the advanced process system or invent one on their own. In other words, the probability that a rival or substitute equalizes the resulting cost advantage over time is always there. The company you are looking at might still make money then, but its outstanding position and enhanced profitability will be gone.

---

[38] Practical knowledge shows that, the more often a task has been performed, the less time is required on each subsequent iteration. Backed by empiricism, the experience curve effect explains gains in efficiency and productivity caused by organisational learning. Generally, the creation of any product or service shows the experience curve effect, with the biggest impact on the absolute costs at the beginning; each time cumulative volume doubles, direct costs per unit fall by a constant percentage.

4. Advantageous Locations

Classically, the value of real estate is derived from three parameters: location, location, and location. It is the location of a house, apartment, or the like that represents the majority of the total property's value from the perspective of private individuals. A nice view from the veranda, a lot of green in the backyard, a good neighbourhood around, infrastructure like grocery shops, hospitals, or schools in the nearby community – you name it. An appealing as well as expedient location is the necessary precondition to be met. That is what normal people basically dream about and pay for in the very first place.

Unsurprisingly, location is a deciding factor for business too. A unique (i.e., advantaged) geographic spot, essential to create a certain customer value, can establish a working barrier to entry towards potential rivals in some industries. An advantageous location represents a structural and wide economic moat that can't be replicated (i.e., overcome) by other economic players. Some businesses have a hard time finding fitting locations for the creation of their products and services, so for the creation of their value propositions. This in turn makes suitable places naturally rare and hence valuable for such parties.

Consequently, the investment process and the related business development function are crucial in such industries. Once the strategic decision is made and the favourable spot is taken, the competitive advantage materialises and becomes structural in nature for the first moving company.

Royal Vopak is one of the world's leading independent tank storage providers for the oil and chemical industries. The company basically offers its customers to store and handle their oil, natural gas, related products and also chemicals in its own facilities at key marine locations around the world. There, Royal Vopak's mission is to ensure safe, reliable, and efficient storage and handling of these hazardous substances which is critical to its customers.

This value proposition requires foremost a geographically advantaged location. The major transport routes of oil and natural gas are structurally pretty much set and stable, which has to do on the one hand with the geographic imbalance between areas of production and areas of consumption of fossil energy and petrochemicals, and on the other hand with the physical nature of oil and gas, asking for a special, careful treatment all along the value chains. Therefore, it would be meaningless to offer the same service at corners that are out of the way somewhere in the world.

The specific location, often a hub location in a harbour along the major distribution ways, is a vital part of Royal Vopak's value proposition. The crucial point is that the strategic location creates at the same time an economic advantage towards rivals for Royal Vopak because such specific spots are quite rare. Spaces in busy harbours are always high in demand and at the same time naturally limited.

Logically, it is the first mover's advantage and the

related investment process that are key for success in this business.[39]

Other examples for businesses with economic moats from advantageous locations might be waste dumps, scrap yards, power stations, or incineration plants. Just from the technical or physical angle, it would make most sense to build them in close distance to the towns and cities where the actual demand comes from. Additional distance means just more transportation costs or a drop in performance as electric tension decreases. But as no one really wants to have a dirty auto graveyard or a fuming power plant in the neighbourhood, the places where such facilities are tolerated by the public and get official approval are reasonably rare. The acceptance from the general public and environmental laws structurally restrict the number of suitable spots for such businesses; this gives the owner of an appropriate location a wide and steadfast economic moat towards potential intruders.

---

[39] Another cardinal part of Royal Vopak's business strategy is about two elements of operational excellence, namely safety and reliability. The related key process "health, security, safety, and environment" encompasses all safety and environmental matters. Safety standards and procedures are set up to mitigate all risks to human life, health, and the environment down to zero. As the value proposition of the firm is to store and handle the customers' goods in a safe and reliable way, the aspects of safety and environmental protection play a central role for Royal Vopak. The negative impact from lethal accidents and pollution would be material. Therefore, unpleasant events must be avoided at all costs. As the potential damages to the customers' reputation would be significant too, the customers are expecting reliable services as well as safe operations at all times and are generally willing to pay a respective price.

To sum up, the initial strategic decision to occupy an exclusive location can create natural mini-monopolies in some geographic areas which after erection are almost not to crack for rivals. The resulting structural cost advantage for the fortunate firm is not global but applies only at local level in geographic terms. But local barriers to entry in turn are not bad. In point of fact, they are the most valuable (i.e., the widest and most durable) economic moats a company can possess in some businesses, just because other firms will literally not be able to slip into such physically occupied markets.

5. Niche Markets / Efficient Scale Effect

The absolute size of markets is structurally set and limited by the demand side. A strict and extreme limitation of the demand size in turn can result in what is commonly called a **niche market**.

In cases when the creation of the respective customer value involves relatively high fixed costs or fixed investments, in the form of high infrastructural investments, general start-up costs, or R&D costs, such markets naturally tend to be just big enough for one company, or at most a handful of firms, which can deliver the product or service most cost efficiently.

In end effect, these two factors - the strict structural limitation of the demand and the naturally occurring cost pattern in an industry - can give rise to a monopolistic or oligopolistic market.

Within such a niche, the (in extreme monopolistic) incumbent generates nice profits while often just manufacturing mundane products or providing unsophisticated services. Potential intruders are discouraged from entering because doing so would cause capital return margins to drop to the floor in the whole market.

The tighter the market is from the demand side and the more capital in the form of fixed spending is needed to start and run the business, the higher are the barriers to entry for the somewhere-lurking rivals.[40] To cover its (fixed) entry costs, the incoming firm would expect a sufficient share of the market. But if the opportunity for that is structurally limited, a ruthless fight for market share is unavoidable. Such a battle, however, is of no good use for any of these firms as it would cause prices to plump and would hurt the returns for all players in the niche.

Of course, this barrier to entry stays and falls with the assumption that potential attackers behave rationally. But as the first mover has already spent shedloads of money in order to be in that business, all potential rivals very likely grasp that the inevitable struggle for shares in that market will be about nothing less than economic survival. Knowing all this and having a certain pricing power in the tight market, the incumbent player often sets prices high enough to generate sufficient returns on invested capital but just low enough to demotivate eventual trespassers.[41]

---

[40] The stakes mount even higher for invasive entities if the required operational assets or knowledge are custom-built or highly specific and, therefore, have no other possible use (i.e., monetary value) except for this particular business.

[41] Heather Brilliant and Elizabeth Collins, *Why Moats Matter: The Morningstar Approach to Stock Investing* (Hoboken, New Jersey: John Wiley & Sons, 2014).

Rationally thinking potential rivals have no real incentive to follow into the constricted and hence unyielding playing field, even if they could; they can already foresee their tiny market shares in the naturally small market, the required long-term spending, the very probable retaliation strategy of the incumbent company, and the devastating consequences for all.

With that, the **efficient scale effect** provides the incumbent firm with a structural and hence strong and durable competitive advantage. All a firm's management needs to do is to identify, open, or occupy the market niche as the first – a strategic task easier said than done, of course.[42]

Coming back to Royal Vopak once more, it is not only a strategically chosen location that is working as an economic moat for this firm. In parallel, Royal Vopak benefits from the structural limitations from the demand side in its markets. Harbours or other hub locations often have just sufficient volume for one or two companies like Royal Vopak at that specific place. Together with the fact that oil, gas, and chemical storage and handling asks for a capital-intensive business model, this externally given limitation of customer demand at certain sites makes the living viable there only for very few players.

---

[42] In principle, niche markets can be developed by a firm from scratch via innovative products and services. In such cases, the new technology does not even need legal protection from a patent or similar means; the market structure works as a reliable economic moat. In other cases, it simply takes a determined and organised move (i.e., an investment in an operational asset like land or machinery) from the company's management into an already existing, unoccupied business field.

Another illustrative example for the efficient scale effect are classic pipelines and related companies.[43] Although the value proposition and the related business model are also neither complicated nor high-tech, firms in this industry sector regularly earn big and sustainable profits on their invested capital.

More importantly, the main reason is simple and structural in nature too. Suppose there is a physical need to get 100 million litres of crude oil per day from an inland oil field to the next refinery. If one pipeline with a capacity of 120 million litres is already built, there is economically no incentive for rivals to enter this market and build another capital-intensive pipeline; the existing pipeline infrastructure is already efficiently scaled to the given market size, not allowing a potential second player enough space in terms of revenues and profits in order to make ends meet.[44]

Because the limitation of the customer demand is one precondition for a niche market, it is easy to guess what can destabilise the exclusive and very profitable position for the lonely but happy incumbent – growth in demand.[45]

Considered normally as something good from

---

[43] Heather Brilliant and Elizabeth Collins, *Why Moats Matter: The Morningstar Approach to Stock Investing* (Hoboken, New Jersey: John Wiley & Sons, 2014).

[44] In addition, the pipeline industry is highly regulated because of environmental and safety aspects. Due to that, governmental regulators prevent the construction of new pipelines unless and until there is a demonstrated and significant economic need to do so. Effectively, the overall barriers to entry in the pipeline industry just get higher.

[45] Bruce Greenwald and Judd Kahn, *Competition Demystified: A Radically Simplified Approach to Business Strategy* (New York: Portfolio, 2007).

firms' and investors' perspectives, the growth of demand in a niche market can harm the financial performance of the incumbent firm by destroying the structural barrier to entry. As the market for the customer value grows, it becomes big enough for more entities to make a proper living. Subsequently, the exclusive position and enhanced profitability for the incumbent gets lost as the market turns from a monopoly or oligopoly to a perfect competition structure amongst rivals. The sheer number of battling companies and the resulting economic pressure in a perfectly competitive market then beat profitability down until the returns on average merely meet the capital costs in that industry.

As an investor, you should look for the risk coming from that direction. You ought to be sure that the addressable market is not only stable but finite at some level of demand. If there is then a significant investment necessary to start and conduct business in such a niche, potential rivals are facing a heavy and structural barrier to entry that is virtually impossible to overcome.

In addition, the management of the incumbent firm can widen and deepen that economic moat even more by keeping its own prices at a modest level. And as the icing on the cake, signalling a credible retaliation strategy to the outside world will finally keep all potential trespassers from spoiling the somehow restricted party.

Being a big frog in a small pond is much better than the opposite. This saying might help you in the future when looking at structurally small markets. And because knowing now about the efficient scale effect and the resulting, powerful economic moat stemming from niche markets, you might also begin to look at the concept of growth from a slightly different angle.

6. Closer Distance and Higher (Local) Density

This meaningful competitive advantage occurs most frequently in industries that are producing raw materials or unprocessed products that are heavy / bulky and cheap, resulting in a low price-to-weight (or price-to-volume) ratio. Transportation costs then become a relatively big cost item in the total product costs, which are in turn a major purchase criterion for the customer. Economically most worthwhile, such goods and products are to be produced in immediate vicinity to where they are consumed or used.

Companies with production facilities located closer to their customers in consequence have almost invariably lower costs, which means that rivals have a hard time cracking their markets. This works especially if a market entry would require significant capital expenditures up front, and hence a long-term commitment, from the potential intruder. But huge investments in plants and machines only make economic sense if the respective firm can expect to get an adequate share of the sales base in a specific area, a precondition that often only holds true for the first mover in the respective (local) market.

Once the first mover is sitting on a decent place near to the customers' final consumption or use, building local density, so scale in a particular geographic area, is the next strategic imperative in order to strengthen the competitive position. By providing the product or good to as many customers as possible, the company uses the local economies of scale to enhance its economic moat. The bigger and denser the customer base becomes in a certain geographic area, the higher the resulting cost advantage (per sales unit) becomes for the incumbent firm, holding potential rivals away from getting a viable foothold in the same region.

With that, the nature of the product and the related transportation cost effect can fundamentally create a (local) mini-monopoly, which extends geographically around the production site.

Companies in bulk industries like LafargeHolcim, a huge manufacturer of building materials such as cement, concrete, and aggregates, possess economic moats of this kind. Growing top line size in order to create economies of scale and driving operational excellence in terms of efficiency and productivity are not enough in this business; producing near to the place of the intended consumption or use is the primary, strategic pillar for such companies' success.

Another example is Praxair, the largest industrial gas company in the Americas measured inter alia in revenues. Its name is derived from a combination of the Greek word "praxis", or practical application, and "air", essentially the company's core product. The company produces and delivers various air gases like oxygen, nitrogen, or hydrogen as well as related technical applications to a wide range of industry customers. These gases and applications are critical for the industry customers as they enable production or enhance efficiency and productivity in their respective operating processes.

Also in the industrial gas business, the key success

factors are the local production and distribution, ultimately due to the physical attributes of Praxair's products or, more precise, the low price-to-weight (or price-to-volume) ratio of the industrial gases. For this reason, local density with respect to the customer portfolio and a related distribution network around a certain production facility represent a strategic imperative for companies like Praxair as well. Once business is in full swing, every additional customer or delivery creates almost no incremental costs for transportation but amplifies the profit margins as the fixed costs are spread over a larger sales base.

But even for companies that do not produce products with a low price-to-weight (or price-to-volume) ratio, a large and dense distribution network can be a valid source of a fairly ample economic moat. Likewise, the delivering process is a major part of the total value from a customer's perspective. The reason lies in the economics at work when moving goods and products from one place to another. Running a distribution network requires definitely tangible assets and very likely also personnel. Therefore, by examining the relation of fixed to variable costs, you would find that the majority of the total costs in the logistics processes are fixed and so not related to the actual output level of the firm.

Let's take a pure logistics company with a fleet of delivery trucks as an example to this. The trucks, as purchased tangible assets, are fixed costs for the firm. The same is true for the salaries of the drivers and the gasoline that the trucks guzzle while they trundle along the entire route. The only real variable costs are overtime wages for busy times and some proportion of the gas if some customers lie far off the optimal route for the main load. Although the initial building and operating of a large and dense delivery network is expensive for the base level of service, the incremental profit the truck fleet can generate is enormous. As soon as the fixed costs are covered, the delivery of each additional item on the route becomes extremely profitable because the variable costs for making an extra stop are almost zero. Imagine now that you would try to contend with a company that has already established a distribution network in a certain area. It likely covers its fixed costs and is making large (incremental) profits as it already delivers tons of materials and thousands of pieces, while you will need to take on large losses for an uncertain period of time till, if ever, you gain enough scale to operate in a profitable manner.

Apparently, many businesses with delivery networks can dig this type of moat; it is not exclusively related to the logistics sector. Restaurant chains, retailers, and also many other companies have all the necessity for moving goods and materials around in order to create their end product or service. The logistics process is a major part of the total value creation process and hence the customer value. Because of that, also these industries or companies have the requirement to install a distribution system that causes mainly fixed costs. Positively for a company, that can become a competitive advantage towards rivals, too. The higher the number of producing or servicing units and the higher the local density within this system, the wider the fixed costs of a distribution network can be spread. In effect, the function logistics within a company get more cost efficient in relation to rivals.

An economic moat from a superior distribution system could be called all management-made, asking a firm's leadership to move (i.e., build) first and to apply organisational talent, but it only works with the basic nature of fixed costs and the relating scale effect, which are naturally given occurrences. As local density and the scale effect go hand in hand and each additional stop or delivery on the route directly leads to more profitability, the moat can widen as well. Once built up, large and dense distribution networks are extremely hard to replicate and are often the source of very extensive and durable competitive advantage towards rivals.

7. Unique Natural Resources

In the energy and basic materials sectors, an advantageous geological deposit can be a formidable source of an economic moat, because humans – even with substantial capital, effort, and time – can't replicate what took Mother Nature millions of years to create.

Some world-class deposits are second to none in grade and size, and an expedient geology normally translates into a favourable stance relative to existing as well potential rivals. If a company is lucky enough to own such a resource deposit with lower (average) extraction costs than any other, it will often have a deciding and enduring economic moat. A unique (i.e., superior) asset can constitute a long-lasting cost advantage for the respective company towards the surrounding rivals.[46]

The all-dominant strategic element for a company comes here again at the very beginning and lies in the identification and purchase of the advantageous asset. Once more, the investment process and the business development function arranged behind it are critical for the company's success. As soon as it's acquired, the access to a unique asset puts a structural advantage up on the cost side for the courageous and determined firm.

The potash mining firm Potash Corporation of Saskatchewan (PotashCorp) is blessed with the biggest and richest resources within its industry. With that, the company is on the low end of the average cost curve, allowing it to earn profits even if potash prices should approach marginal costs of the industry's average production in the future.

The lower (average) costs stem from the geology and natural size of the firm's Canadian deposits. And although the production costs per unit are further driven down by maximising output and related scale effects, PotashCorp would not be in its profitable position if the potash resources were not that unique / superior in their richness and mass.

But unique natural resources do not only impress with their pure size and quantities. Further physical attributes can also make natural assets superior to others.

The technologies of hydraulic fracturing, or fracking, and directional drilling have made energy

---

[46] Tim Koller, Richard Dobbs, and Bill Huyett, *Value: The Four Cornerstones of Corporate Finance* (Hoboken, New Jersey: John Wiley & Sons, 2011).

sources available that were not in reach before. In the United States and Canada, these new properties are rich and have led to a real boom for shale energy resources in recent years, which came up already in the 1990s. However, with these new players big in business, the whole oil and natural gas market structure started to change a few years ago.[47]

Before, OPEC[48] used to be an oligopoly that could steer prices while adjusting volume. But with the new massive supply in the market, the oligopoly structure did not function anymore. To make an oligopoly work, the members must act in concert and be able to control the vast majority of the total market volume. OPEC saw its inability to keep up its oligopolistic regime and did not want to kind of subsidize the US shale resources by its own discipline within the cartel either. The OPEC members, with Saudi Arabia as the dominating leader, were therefore forced to boost production in order to keep their market share and to fight their, on average, more expensive rivals from

---

[47] Fracking and directional drilling represent classic examples for disruptive technologies that can completely transform an industry environment and the respective capitalistic game within. Clayton M. Christensen, *The Innovator's Dilemma: The Revolutionary Book that Will Change the Way You Do Business* (New York: HarperBusiness Essentials, 2003).

[48] The Organization of the Petroleum Exporting Countries (OPEC) was founded in Baghdad, Iraq, with the signing of an agreement in September 1960 by five countries, namely the Islamic Republic of Iran, Iraq, Kuwait, Saudi Arabia, and Venezuela. The mission of OPEC is to coordinate and unify the petroleum policies of its member countries and, furthermore, to ensure the stabilisation of the oil markets in order to secure an efficient, economic, and regular supply of petroleum to consumers, a steady income to producers, and a fair return on capital for those investing in the petroleum industry.

North America.

The new market form nowadays is, as in many industries and for the benefit of the end consumers, a perfectly competitive market between rivals, where prices are determined solely by supply and demand; consequently, the incumbent firms produce their individual and cost-optimal volume in relation to that market price.

So it is not that OPEC masterminded a "brilliant" plan to defeat its rivals – it had no choice but it was lucky to hit the new rivals pretty hard.[49] Many shale energy players produce at relatively high costs and need respective high oil and natural gas prices in order to make a living. And although the new technology and the experience curve effect still drive down the average costs of supply, many shale resource plays will not deliver sustainable results at the new price levels in the transformed market environment.

But the significant depression of oil and natural gas prices in this day and age is just a reflection of a temporary oversupply. As a consequent and harsh reaction to the new state of affairs, the oil majors have cut costs and have already stopped many of their greenfield investments. At the end, shareholders want to have enduring success, and banks want to see balance sheets in order. And because the oil and natural gas business not only is quite capital-intensive but normally also takes some time to ramp up new

---

[49] Simultaneously, also the main substitutes of oil and gas, namely coal as well as renewable energies, have been thwarted; they are economically much less competitive at the low oil and gas price levels of the years 2015 and 2016.

capacities, it is just a matter of time before prices will again trend north as the current supply will naturally dry up. It is then the times of high prices, and the corresponding pain at the petrol pump for the car drivers, when the whole industry has again money to invest, which in turn results in higher supply and lower prices. All in all, assuming a constant demand and shale energy also existing in the future, the oil and natural gas markets will show the typical price swings of capital-intensive commodity markets.[50]

Going forward, it will then be the most flexible producers with the lowest cost of supply that will make the lion's share of potential profits in such an economic environment.

ConocoPhillips is currently the largest independent exploration and production firm in the oil and natural gas industry. This company is in possession of special shale oil and natural gas wells, besides other energy resources, in North America. And here is the key point – oil is not oil if looking at the cost of supply curves and other characteristics of the resources.

ConocoPhillips controls many sweet spots in the lower forty-eight[51] and Canada, some of the most secure, flexible and cheapest energy sources in the world. As you can see from this example, it is not

---

[50] This scenario holds true even if OPEC could ally itself with strong non-OPEC members like Russia in a reliable manner. The additional amount of oil and gas, available today at certain price levels and thanks to the new exploration technologies, is just too huge and not in control of the cartel. Unfortunate for OPEC, it is in the hands of many independent countries as well as private companies that will likely not join sustainable agreements about production rates.

[51] Continental United States of America, excluding Hawaii and Alaska as well as all off-shore US territories and possessions.

necessarily always only the magnitude of a natural resource that provides a company with a competitive advantage. ConocoPhillips is in a commanding position regarding profitability within its industry due to other qualities of its energy resource plays – safety, adaptability, and low-cost accessibility.

Although global demand is still slightly on the rise, the new market environment has led to a lower and more volatile price environment in the oil and natural gas industry. This new economic system calls for new key success factors, and ConocoPhillips has them all. The uniqueness of its natural resources gives this firm a structural cost advantage compared to most rivals within the new market environment.

The take-away from here is clear: while watching for economic moats from unique (i.e., superior) natural resources, you should consider not only size and quantities but also specifics such as the initial exploration costs, grade, security, and flexibility. Above all, the ultimate question you should keep in mind and clarify is always how cost-competitive and reliable the geological deposits or other natural resources are compared to the peers and substitutes.

8. Better Application and Compliance Processes

The capitalistic game, as described earlier, does not happen in an empty space. Capitalism (i.e., competition) needs an institutional frame to unleash its positive power and to tame its dark sides. Companies need rules and shelter at the same time in order to conduct business in a proper and safe way.[52] No company should do business at the expense of the environment, workforce, or other, unrelated parties.

Governmental regulations are set to ensure environmental sustainability, technical safety, and fair working conditions in all industries. Hence, companies that want to start working often first have to undergo official approval processes. And even after receiving the initial approvals and necessary official permits, while companies are actually doing business, the government regularly asks for legal compliance in many respects. Consequently, to overcome and fulfil all the regulatory hurdles and legal requirements, not only are a smooth application process and related management skills mandatory but so is operational excellence in terms of reliable compliance with the respective laws.

The banking and insurance sectors might be good examples where compliance really matters. As the overall regulation frame in these industries has tightened quite a bit over the last few years, it will be the financial institutions with proper compliance processes and an effective corporate governance system in place that will do best in the reformed economic system.

Economic moats from governmental regulation regarding environment protection laws or labour rights function best (i.e., are most durable) if there is a bunch of small-scale rules, rather than one big rule, that can be surprisingly changed by government or,

---

[52] Raghuram G. Rajan and Luigi Zingales, *Saving Capitalism from the Capitalists: Unleashing the Power of Financial Markets to Create Wealth and Spread Opportunity* (New Jersey: Princeton University Press, 2004).

at least same important, can be more easily followed by rivals in the same way.⁵³

Take the agricultural sector as an example. Although the overall success and the major differentiator of Monsanto, a world-scale developer and maker of advanced agricultural and vegetable seeds, bio technologic traits, and crop protection chemicals, is based on new technology, innovation, and the corresponding patents, the constant change of the regulation in its business field is also a source for competitive advantages towards peers.

Regulatory hurdles for a new product are already high in the Western world and are tending to get even higher; additional study requirements are just one of the consequences for the companies in this industry. The respective governmental bodies ask all companies to participate in long and cumbersome approval processes and to comply with all sorts of tests and standards, even for existing products.

All this finally creates not only a structural burden in but also a barrier to entry to this industry; only the companies with long experience and working processes in these matters will master the challenge. Knowing ex ante what documentation and legal procedures are mandatory helps to avoid costly product withdrawals and lawsuits. In other words, as the possibilities for non-approval, trials, and product withdrawals constitute material risks inherent in this business, respective operating processes can help to efficiently and reliably manage such jeopardies,

---

[53] Pat Dorsey, *The Little Book that Builds Wealth: The Knockout Formula for Finding Great Investments* (Hoboken, New Jersey: John Wiley & Sons, 2008).

leading the best-in-class company to a solid cost advantage compared to its rivals.

Furthermore, the relating economic moat is most potent when a regulatory approval to operate in a market is stipulated but the company is not subject to economic oversight with regard to how it prices its products or services within these boundaries. Or expressed more straight-forwardly, the regulatory hurdles to receive official approval for a product or service (i.e., to get into a market) are high but once in, no further regulatory pressure is exercised by the government on the incumbents. If you can find a company that can price and act like a monopoly without really being regulated like one, you have probably found a company with a wide economic moat. Monsanto represents such companies, but this circumstance applies for many pharmaceutical corporations too.

Another area for economic moats from a superior application process and reliable compliance are **licences**, **concessions**, and **exploitation rights** issued by the government. Examples where one big licence is needed from and given by the government in an auction process are the telecommunication sector or the casino operator industry.[54]

The application or tendering process and related management expertise are of paramount importance if a licensing arrangement with the government comes under the hammer via an auction process. Legal expertise and compliance are necessary, and

---

[54] Heather Brilliant and Elizabeth Collins, *Why Moats Matter: The Morningstar Approach to Stock Investing* (Hoboken, New Jersey: John Wiley & Sons, 2014).

experience from other business areas can help as well; all that is management input. But once the highly coveted right is won, the respective firm can enjoy the fact that it does not have to fight hard anymore with anyone for the customers' favour; the competitive pressure from peers is blocked for the contracted time frame.

So, in general, a licence, concession, or exploitation right builds a structural shield towards potential intruders for a while and constitutes a (temporary) monopoly-like position for the respective firm that wins the respective bid.

Besides this, also in the private sector, a better application or tendering process can matter and bring out an economic moat for some firms. For service providers that do operations and maintenance for others' property, such as operators on an airport, or that work on others' premises, like the drilling service companies for the big oil majors, the bidding for new contracts is an inherent, crucial part of the business model. Also in these businesses, the application or bidding process requires management talent and steady focus. To work as a barrier to entry, the final contract must result in an exclusive relation with the customers; that way, it effectively shields the respective company for some time from external rivalry.

As you might have noticed, apart from the elaborated cost advantages, in some cases a regulatory approval, license, or successful bid work pretty much like a patent and have a similar, positive effect on the respective firm's revenues (via higher and more stable sales prices as well as volumes).

In conclusion, please see that barriers to entry from a better application or tendering process compared to peers as well as the reliable compliance to related regulations or laws can provide relative cost advantages and can give solid, although only temporary, shelter from rivals' attacks.

But there are also really negative aspects to mention here. The margins for all participating companies can get pulverised in a tendering process if the fight for a contract, license, or the like becomes suicidal; one unreasonable bidder can make the whole business unprofitable. Apart from that, a competitive advantage from the application and compliance processes requires never-stopping efforts from management. It needs skilled, full-time attention from a firm's leadership, not only in the formation phase of the business but on an ongoing basis. And as management action can always be copied more easily than physical (i.e., structural) conditions, the risk that the elaborated competitive advantage vanishes at some point in time is definitely there.

Please just recognise these drawbacks and dangers when analysing a company, and make your own call then.

IV. Negotiation Power along the Value Chain

Dominating Customers and Suppliers

As described earlier, the concept of competition also encloses the customers and the suppliers of a firm right along its value chain. These economic parties also try to maximise their negotiation power and profits in the capitalistic game.

All competitive advantages described in this chapter ultimately bring the respective company into a superior position to negotiate prices, terms, and conditions with its customers as well as its suppliers.

Economies of scale and scope play for a second time a vital role, bringing the possessing company into a dominating position via sheer size or a well-composed variety of business activities.

Switching costs represent a powerful competitive advantage too, working as a barrier to leave and forcing the customers to stick with a certain company's products or services.

In strong contrast to this, also some other effects establish barriers to leave for the customers but are functioning in a kind of positive way. Brands and the network effect are competitive advantages that eventually create loyalty, making the customers actually want to buy only the products or services of one particular firm.

Last but not least, structural negotiation power for a firm, especially towards its customers, can stem from an unspectacular but mighty detail. Let me start my further explanations with this latter, maybe somewhat surprising, effect.

Relative Small Prices

Pricing power and active domination of terms and conditions are actually what we are after at the end of the day when searching for companies with high negotiation power towards their customers.

So pricing power due to the fact that the company's product or service demands only a relative small portion of the customer's cost budget or income is highly welcome, although it has something special. The pricing power from this stated reason is a structural phenomenon, most often deeply rooted in a firm's value proposition and the related business model. Hence, such a company gets naturally in a good position when it comes to pricing. Small prices in relative terms allow a company to raise prices even in difficult times with immediate effect on revenues and profitability. The customers, be these private individuals or professional companies, are not likely to rebel against such action because, from their perspective, it is just not worth the fight regarding time or money. In many cases, they do not even notice the impact from inflated prices in absolute terms in their pockets.

In order to grasp how critical this structural competitive advantage is, you might recall my points made about pricing in tendering processes. In the construction business or the aircraft manufacturing industry, for instance, the price of the company's product or service is regularly such a material amount that the customers invest considerable time and effort to really get the lowest prices and finest terms available in the market. These industries are undoubtedly lacking the effect from relative small prices, which structurally puts a heavy weight on their margins and profitability.

To spot companies benefiting from the said competitive advantage, you just need to look around you. Every day, you buy several, little items at relative small prices. The immateriality of the amount from your angle, at the very point of purchase, makes you unaware about the (relative) pricing of such goods and services. This is what companies know and hence exploit. Chewing gum might be one classic example for the effect from relative small prices. And there are way more. Snacks, lighters, ball-point pens, razors, screws, cleansers, cosmetics – a lot of unimposing products create good, sometimes even crucial values every day while not being pretty expensive relative to a consumer's total budget.

In business-to-business relationships, industrial gases from Praxair and satellite communication solutions from SES Global[55] represent permanently, vitally needed products and services, respectively, for

---

[55] Headquartered in Luxembourg, SES Global is a world-leading satellite operator, providing reliable and secure satellite communication solutions to broadcast, telecom, corporate, and government customers. According to the company's own statement, it technically can connect its customers with 99 percent of the world's population through its far-reaching infrastructure and services; in the financial year 2015, it generated roughly $ 2.2 billion of revenues and $ 1.6 billion of EBITDA.

relative small money per unit from the customers' standpoints.

Altogether, relative small prices represent a structural competitive advantage that a lucky company likely shares with its entire industry. Nevertheless, this fact enhances the negotiation power of such blessed firms via pricing by some margin points and subsequently has a considerable effect on their profitability.

Combined with an essential and frequent demand for a certain product or service, a competitive advantage from relative small prices can constitute the corpus of a very remunerative business. That's why when you analyse a particular company next time, you should check on this tiny but valuable aspect as well.

Size / Economies of Scale

Whereas size in revenue terms can, under some conditions, constitute a barrier to entry for rivals and substitutes, it enhances a firm's negotiation power along the value chain towards its customers as well as its suppliers without any major qualification.

Due to its broad product portfolio, PepsiCo, for instance, has not only cost advantages relative to peers in the form of economies of scope in some of its central processes like marketing, but also (combined) economies of scale directly along its value chain. In other words, the different revenue streams of PepsiCo translate along the value chain into a "combined scale" advantage towards its customers. Not that every single product category is already enormous by itself; the revenue streams of the different products just tot up to a colossal block when it comes to negotiations with some customers like the big retailers. The snacks and beverages behemoth has a vast selection of formidable brands in its product portfolio. Chips and soda are normally purchased and consumed together. As high-impulse buys or basket builders, such food and beverage categories cause traffic in the stores. But juices and Quaker oats are also high in demand and generate steady revenues for PepsiCo as well as the retailers. PepsiCo can use this broad as well as deep sales base in its negotiations with retailing giants like Walmart or Costco. When PepsiCo and Walmart, for instance, sit at the table to discuss terms and conditions, that meeting happens on the same eye level. As a matter of fact, in this relationship, Walmart can't just dictate things. It has to talk with PepsiCo not only about prices but also about other interesting facets of the overall contract, like minimum purchase quantities, product presentation, or shelf space.

With the Kraft Heinz Company, it is basically the same story. When the investment firms 3G Capital and Berkshire Hathaway teamed up few years ago to shape a new conglomerate through the merger of the H. J. Heinz Company and the Kraft Foods Group, they effectively formed the fifth-largest food company in the world and the third-largest in the United States.[56]

Thereby, the new big player in the food industry, the Kraft Heinz Company, has significant synergies on

---

[56] According to the company's own statement in 2015 after the merger, it holds (inter alia) eight distinct food brands, each valued at $ 1 billion or more, based on retail sales.

the cost side as well as advantages from the combined size of all its various revenue streams together. The latter aspect (i.e., the sum of all the sales volumes united under one roof) inevitably results in more negotiation power towards customers like large retail outlets, specialty food stores, or restaurants regarding better prices, delivery and payment terms on average, more shelf space, and the like. Due to the global footprint of Heinz products, the merger will also help to sell more Kraft products in international markets; the collective size of the newly formed food giant just pushes doors open. Besides this aspect there were likely many other rationales and motivations for this merger – but the combined scale was sure enough a big one of them.

In addition, size does matter big time when looking at the upper part of the total value chain. Towards suppliers, a company's scale directly translates into purchasing power. Especially in businesses where competition between rivals is perfect and sales prices are a given (market) parameter, lower input costs due to enhanced negotiation power towards the suppliers represent a vital source of profits for the acting companies.

The cocoa and chocolate business of Barry Callebaut is primarily volume-driven. And the more Barry Callebaut produces and sells, the more input in the form of raw materials like cocoa beans, milk, and sugar it needs.

Generally, because a big purchase also triggers economies of scale for the supplier, it is just a reasonable behaviour of the ordering company to demand some share of that benefit in the form of price discounts or the like. So by having purchasing power mainly derived from superior size in sales, Barry Callebaut can ask, for example, the cocoa bean suppliers for much lower prices than anybody else in its industry.

Apart from this, size helps the firm not only to realise better wholesale prices but also to get better qualities and other favourable conditions. For example, by having negotiated long-term delivery contracts with many agricultural cooperative societies for cocoa directly, Barry Callebaut can effectively mitigate its operational risk of supply bottlenecks.

Taken all together, its size helps Barry Callebaut to enhance return and to reduce risk at the same time.

The same goes in principle for the big automobile manufacturers like Toyota or Volkswagen as well. Because they procure steel as a major raw material for their motor vehicles in huge quantities, they can of course expect better prices and terms when talking to the steel mills than smaller rivals or a small factory for pots and pans. Steel mills like ArcelorMittal or thyssenkrupp are by themselves capital-intensive, commodity-like businesses where size and the related economies of scale translate in a straight line into their major competitive advantage towards peers as well as substitutes.

With that, these suppliers to the car industry economically benefit from larger orders as well and hence are generally willing to give the top conditions to their biggest customers.

Synergies / Economies of Scope

From a company's point of view, variety in the product or service portfolio has negative and positive aspects – more complexity and inflexibility on the downside, higher negotiation power on the upside. As described in the previous chapter, being able to rein complexity and inflexibility can bring a company in a favourable position compared to its rivals from a cost perspective. But companies that produce a multiplicity of products or deliver a range of services can also put themselves in a very nice position directly towards their customers and suppliers.

First, combining various revenue streams or business areas in a smart way, as described in the previous section, translates into a "combined scale" advantage and resulting negotiation power for a company towards its customers, taking the assumption that all products or services offered are relevant for the same customer. Of course, only if one particular customer has real interest in the whole portfolio, the respective company can use this combined size of sales volume in the negotiations.

In a similar fashion, scope works towards the supplier side too. The purchasing power of a firm towards its suppliers can stem from economies of scope, so the pooling of different business segments and related buying processes, but only if the collective amounts of raw materials or input factors are demanded from the same suppliers.

When Dow Chemical and DuPont announced a merger of equals in late 2015, economies of scope were one of the main rationales behind the deal. The general intent of the management is to split the new conglomerate after the merger into three independent, publicly traded companies and to create three new industry leaders, namely in the business fields of agriculture, materials, and specialty products. Each of them will not only possess more size in single-product or single-service categories by just bringing together the overlapping business activities but also possess a more encompassing and hence complete product and service portfolio overall. Via the liaison of different but highly complementing business activities, each of these new companies will have economies of scope and related cost advantages towards their rivals, accompanied by enhanced importance and negotiation power towards customers as well as suppliers along the value chain. In total, it is expected to unlock circa $ 3 billion of cost synergies and approximately an additional $ 1 billion in revenue growth synergies through this transaction.

Second, companies with a broad product or service portfolio can offer a more comprehensive value proposition out of the same hand, which might be convenient for the customers. In extreme, though, some well-positioned companies have such a widespread product or service portfolio that they can actually completely circumvent their traditional customers.

Companies like Samsung or LG are in the first place manufacturers of consumer electronics. But by having such a broad value proposition with a plethora of products in place, ranging from basic consumer goods such as washing machines, dishwashers, refrigerators, or air conditioners to high-end electronic devices like smartphones, laptops, and the latest generation of TV, these companies can simply bypass the big retailers, their natural customers, via their own stores and target the end consumers directly. In their own outlets, Samsung or LG are in immediate interaction with their ultimate customers and can present their products or services the way they want to. Having no traditional retailer as an intermediary anymore on the distribution way normally augments the producing companies' overall capital return margins.

Also, Nike and Adidas, international companies that are traditionally engaged in the design, development, and manufacturing of sportswear, athletic shoes, sports equipment, and related accessories, apply such a distribution strategy for the exact same reasons. End consumers are generally easier to deal with from a negotiation point of view than the big retailers. Even in this day and age of the Internet, individuals are less organised and informed than professional companies. Most importantly, however, individuals make the more emotional buying decisions. Rather than calculating conservatively and comparing objectively, human beings tend to trust their gut feelings when it comes to a product's value and the price for it. The less information is available and the more emotions are attached to an item or the situation, the more the final choice rests on feelings. Apart from that, emotions in this context can be part of the whole value proposition for which the customers are actually willing to pay for.

But all this does not hold true for every company. Setting up and running a chain of stores of course also costs money and comes with a new set of risks for a producer. Therefore, although an "own store" concept enables a producing company to present its value proposition directly and tailor-made to its chosen core customers, the respective management needs to consider the economic cons for such a distribution system too. Only if the direct access to the ultimate consumers results in a risk-adequate increase in profitability can economies of scope create value for the respective company this way.

Switching Costs

Assuming customers in principle have a choice in a market, switching costs are their net burden in order to change from one producer or provider to another. As a rule, you find the effect of switching costs if the burden in the form of time, effort, risk, or money to change from one product or service to another weighs heavier than the benefit of doing so. Customers just get stuck with the currently used product or service due to the switching costs.

Therefore, switching costs and the resulting customer captivity represent a valuable competitive advantage from a company's perspective. The customers can't easily drop the existing business relationship with a certain company in order to switch at low costs or in a hassle-free manner to an alternative product or service. Due to switching costs in its products or services, a company has more negotiation power towards its customers and can charge more money or ask for better terms than it could without such barriers to leave.

Switching costs stem by and large from structural reasons resting in the industry environment and the general value creation process itself. Hence, they predominantly come into sight at industry level, in most cases for all incumbent firms towards their (end) customers. Of course, if a whole industry commonly applies a similar business approach, you might be in temptation to consider switching costs as a kind of custom-made strategy. But (good) strategy was defined earlier as the individual answer of one firm to competitive pressure, firstly towards direct rivals. In this definition, strategy means that a single company follows its own distinct approach, trying to separate from other peers and holding substitutes at bay.

To be honest, creating switching costs via an individual strategy is pretty hard for any single company. As switching costs are in principle something negative for the customers, a firm's strategy that strives to impose or enhance switching costs for the clientele in a too noticeable way either will be soon countered by another firm that offers the customer value in a more customer-friendly way or will suffer retaliation strategies from its customers over time.

In many end consumer-oriented industries such as retailing, restaurants, or airlines, switching costs for the customers structurally tend to be almost zero. You can easily put yourself in the shoes of the customers from your own experience. No one stops you walking from one clothing store to another, spontaneously trying another eatery, or booking a different airline each time you fly into the sun. It requires no time, effort, risk, or money to switch a product or service within each of these circumstances. In such industries, the investor would need to look then for distinct strategies of the firms to construct some customer captivity.

For instance, retailers regularly try to induce their customers with vouchers after a buy or loyalty bonuses to come back another time. Sweetened with the promise of a discount on the next shopping, this tactic imposes a light and subtle kind of switching costs for the retailers' clientele.

Airlines, to pick another example, also face structurally low switching costs but have not found so far a good strategic answer to that challenge either. The ease with which customers can switch from one carrier to another on popular routes makes it hard for airlines to raise prices or cut service levels. In the days of the Internet, the customer is just one click away from the rivals' offering or a substitute like the railway. Frequent-flyer programs and marketing campaigns were intended to raise customer captivity somewhat, but they have not been effective to the magnitude hoped for.

Apparently, there are also more successful tactics to establish switching costs for the customers. Elevators or printers can serve as examples where customers, private or professional ones, get a low entry price for the main physical product but have to pay quite hefty bills for maintenance services, repairs, and spare parts. To some extent, the respective firms lure their customers into a kind of trap.

You can observe this kind of "sneaking in" tactic also for some plain consumer goods like razors or electric tooth-brushes. It is actually not the main part of the total product system that is expensive but the spare parts like the razor blades or the brush heads.

But once the initial purchase is made by the customers, it gets relatively costly and mentally cumbersome for them to switch again to another product; hence, the people have to stick to what they originally bought.

Banks and insurance companies have been long time good examples for industries with structurally high switching costs for their customers. To quit one bank relationship and start with another or to switch an insurance coverage provider used to be a laborious and lengthy procedure in the older days. But banks and insurance companies lost dramatically on their structural advantages from switching costs when the Internet came up. Due to the revolutionary technology, customers were able to switch bank accounts and insurance policies without any big effort, time, or costs anymore.

Yet although the bank and insurance industries have faced tough headwinds since the Internet has made it very convenient for customers to inform, compare, and switch to respective peers at no costs, their industry environments still create some switching costs that help all firms in the financial industry to keep a proper negotiation position towards the customers.[57]

---

[57] People have very often the general tendency to stick with their current, suboptimal situation although a change to the better would not cost too much in terms of time and money. This **status quo bias** is caused by very human behaviour patterns like lack of attention, phlegm, as well as loss aversion. Richard H. Thaler and Cass R. Sunstein, *Nudge: Improving Decisions about Health, Wealth, and Happiness* (New York: Penguin Books, 2009).

As you might realise at this point, also the competitive advantage from switching costs is not a carved-in-stone thing; it can strengthen or weaken when the industry environment structurally changes (e.g., when new technologies evolve or the underlying customer demand alters).

Imposing switching costs in pure business-to-business industries is even harder. The customer is not a private individual who wants to maximise his or her overall well-being but a professional, profit-oriented organisation. Every company strictly aims for having low switching costs, or the other way around, high degrees of freedom. Being unbound to others helps companies to make unrestricted and flexible decisions, especially in hard times. Low switching costs are hence a strategic imperative or an inherent part of the risk management strategy for every firm in order to prevent economic dependence on its suppliers that play the capitalistic game too. This underlying motivation to minimise the suppliers' negotiation power is the main reason why switching costs for an industry customer on a permanent basis due to another firm's strategy are rare, especially if the delivered good or service is a commodity-like product or service. Every company is constantly on the watch, trying to overcome, if possible, all dependencies that force it to do something without a real benefit in return.

Nevertheless, one worthwhile business strategy directly aimed at customer captivity and the relating switching costs in business-to-business relations can be the integration of the providing firm into the (industry) customer's business processes. As no commercial undertaking likes to get limited in its degrees of freedom for nothing or even worse, the only way a company can create switching costs for its (industry) customers without effecting immediate resistance is to offer additional customer value in exchange.

Linde, as a case in point, follows such a strategic approach to erect switching costs for its industry customers. This group is, like Praxair, a leading industrial gases and engineering company with international operations. Linde has around sixty-five thousand employees and is represented in more than one hundred countries worldwide – a true global player.

Especially in its merchant business line (i.e., the supply of industrial gases in cylinders or in bulk via trucks) switching costs structurally are low. Therefore, the company started delivering more than only the plain molecules. Linde delivers additional value in the form of technical applications that get fixed installed within the customers' production processes. Providing such custom-tailored solutions generates higher value than pure molecule supply and, maybe even more critically, crafts customer captivity. The range of Linde's industry customers is widespread, and so are the examples for technical applications. An appliance for the automobile industry customers, for instance, uses carbon dioxide as feedstock from Linde in order to produce dry ice.[58]

---

[58] The naturally occurring chemical compound carbon dioxide, chemical formula CO_2, is a colourless, odourless gas vital to life on earth. The frozen, solid form of CO_2, known as dry ice, is used amongst other things as a refrigerant or as an abrasive in dry ice-blasting technologies.

With that medium, the apparatus cleans surfaces of cars before painting and coating. The customer economises time due to faster production flows and realises cost savings due to less waste of water as well as decreased energy usage. The mentioned Linde system also requires less space and fewer process steps than other available technologies. In another case, Linde developed special burners for the glass industry. Physically integrated in the manufacturing processes and fed with Linde's gases, this equipment optimises productivity, efficiency, and, last not but least, the quality of the customers' utile and beautiful end products.

In effect, customers using Linde's technical applications show higher loyalty. This is to some extent because it is costly, timely, and complicated to remove the devices once installed at the customer's site. The physical connection and synchronisation with a Linde apparatus sets a very high and durable barrier to leave for the respective customer. But to even that limitation out in a way, Linde's solutions help the customers to enhance their own production processes as well as operational excellence, and the end products themselves. Therefore, the total customer value increases as well - a win-win situation for Linde and its customers.

And so while creating additional customer value with its technology-driven strategy, Linde builds for itself a durable competitive advantage in the form of lasting and meaningful switching costs for its industry clients, bringing the company into a better position to negotiate prices and terms. In 2014, circa 40 percent of Linde's merchant revenues were driven by technical applications and solutions tailored to practical customer needs.

Let me give you a brief recap and some final advice regarding this competitive advantage.

It is generally difficult for any company to take its customers as prisoners by building up switching costs for them; no customer likes to be out of choice, and a customer will try to get around such inflexibility by all means. Yet companies eagerly try in many ways to lock their customers up somehow because this enables them to negotiate better prices and terms with a positive effect on their own profitability and risk profiles. As a competitive advantage, switching costs for the customers just help big time to improve and stabilise the ROIC of the respective firm.

The best way for a firm to achieve customer captivity in this regard is definitely by means of offering additional value in exchange. In the ideal situation, the customer becomes captive to the providing firm without actually wanting to escape. Propelled by new technology and innovation, some companies like Linde deliver long-term customer value while firmly chaining themselves to their customers at the same time.

So apart from searching for industries that possess structural switching costs (e.g., like the elevator / escalator sector), it can be worthwhile for you as an investor to look out for single companies that have efficaciously created switching costs via a distinct, clever business strategy.

Brands

Especially in the classic end-consumer markets, where the actual final users are the customers to be convinced, switching costs to other products or services on the one hand and the barriers to entry for rivals and substitutes to the relevant market on the other hand are all low.

In such cases, a brand is then most often the only way to create an advantageous position for an incumbent firm towards its customers. Due to their very nature, brands as a source of competitive advantages are weightier in the end user oriented, business-to-consumer sectors rather than in the business-to-business sectors.

In order to generate customer captivity in a positive way (i.e., via loyalty), a brand must be founded on something that is meaningful for the customers; it must transport a clear and exclusive value that exists in the customers' perception. Such customer value can stem from positive emotions or a better taste attached to the buy or the consumption. A brand can also give the customers a personal style or image, accentuate individuality, or indicate a certain social standing. Apart from this, the customers can benefit from the signalling function a brand has; a brand can give orientation and security. As the customers can expect, backed by personal experience, certain quality standards attached to a brand, searching costs decrease, and the final purchase decision gets easier.[59]

Nonetheless, one of the most common misunderstandings is to assume that every well-known brand automatically endows its owner with a competitive advantage. In fact, nothing could be further from the truth. A brand originates negotiation power for the possessing firm only if it increases the consumer's willingness to pay more or affects regular buys. Only if the customer (subjectively) experiences a meaningful and durable value will the brand also create value for the providing firm. An investor should never mix up plain **brand awareness**, or the general publicity of a brand, with true **brand power**, the real force of attraction from a brand.

Therefore, when examining a company with a well-known consumer brand – or one that argues that its brand is valuable within a certain relevant market – ask yourself whether the company is able to charge a premium relative to similar competing products or to sell more than comparable firms at the same price level. If not, that brand may not be worth very much from the respective company's perspective. After all, to build and sustain a brand costs a lot of the management's effort, time, and money. But if such investments do not generate an appropriate return via some pricing power or repeat business, driven by the customers' preferences or habits, they are not creating any value for the company's investors, either. So it is true-life brand loyalty that we as

---

[59] M. G. Parameswaran, *Building Brand Value: Five Steps to Building Powerful Brands* (New Delhi: Tata McGraw-Hill Publishing Company Limited, 2006).

investors want to see. Only if a brand verifiably makes customers buy more frequently and regularly or take heftier prices for granted do we factually have a valuable brand in front of us.

Take Sony, for example. This Japanese firm is definitely a global company and legendary brand, known for decades for its stylish and good-quality electronic devices. Now ask yourself if you would pay more for a DVD player solely because it has the Sony name on it, while comparing it to a DVD player with similar features and guaranteed quality standards from Philips, Samsung, or Panasonic. Odds are good that you would not – at least the majority of people would not, according to some commercial surveys – because technical facets and prices generally matter more to consumers when buying most kinds of basic electronics than brands do.[60]

Another industry where brands within the industry do not count too much is the credit card business. People rely on certain standards that are basically guaranteed by law. So a brand is not necessary to give customers that confidence. Apart from that, credit card users just want to be sure that they can pay their bills in every restaurant, shop, or hotel in the world. A brand does not signal or guarantee that. People check the value proposition of American Express, Visa, or Master Card and then make a buying decision based on the objective features offered to them. Last but not least, not really many people would

---

[60] Pat Dorsey, *The Little Book that Builds Wealth: The Knockout Formula for Finding Great Investments* (Hoboken, New Jersey: John Wiley & Sons, 2008).

opt for one or the other credit card in order to appear to be stylish or special. And if some do, all credit card companies can offer the same platinum or gold card standard in order to satisfy egos to the same extent. With all that, and although all these credit card companies are highly known around the globe, it is not their brands in the first place that make them so prosperous.

Also, many airlines and logistics companies are well-known by the majority of the population. But not too many people will choose one of them because of their brands. Again, as service levels are more or less equal across rivals, the price is for most customers the main factor for the final buying decision.

Let us now turn to companies that do indeed expose real brand power. Nike and Apple are companies with iconic brands. Everyone knows these companies and relates their names directly to their products. In addition, many people prefer Nike or Apple compared to their respective rivals and are willing to pay a premium for their products and services.

Quality, technical features, a personal lifestyle statement, social standing - Nike and Apple promise and deliver all these values for their customers and hence undeniably possess brand power. You just need to compare Nike's or Apple's pricing, sales volume and profitability with their known peers in order to clearly see that.

Generally, customer loyalty and related competitive advantages from brands are purely management-made. It necessitates not one but many ingredients to create a brand with real drawing power, and one of them might also be a good portion of luck, as always in life.

But foremost and as mentioned a little earlier, a brand must stand for solid values in the customers' eyes – ideally for an everlasting value like high quality, decent image, or good taste. No marketing campaign on earth can sustainably stick a certain value to a brand that is actually not there; consumers are just not that stupid in the long run.

To build sustainable values from brands requires not necessarily being the first mover in a certain market. Hence, playing only the second fiddle or starting from scratch in a market might work fine for an upcoming, fresh company. But what it definitely needs is a compelling product or service, a relentless and skilled management focus and, therefore, a good and consistent business strategy. The establishment of a certain perception in the customer's memory is difficult and laborious not only at the very beginning but also during the whole life of the product or service. It takes years to set up a powerful brand - but just seconds to destroy it.

And as consumers' tastes and desires can change, sometimes pretty fast, the respective firm's management in turn is forced to relentlessly check how the consumers' preferences develop and eventually alter. If the tastes and desires of the core customers change, the product and its related brand hopefully can adapt to that, still imposing a meaningful customer value. If not, the brand inevitably loses its meaning for the consumers and, with that, also its value for the owning firm.

To see brands that are temporarily powerful but quite often do not effect a durable competitive advantage, you just have to look at the fashion industry.

Brands in the fashion industry stand for style, chic, luxury, or exclusivity. These are clearly values for many individuals. But trends in fashion come and go very quickly. This roots in the value proposition itself. People want to appear to be special and to underscore their individuality, so fashion constantly needs to change in order to deliver these customer values. If customers lose interest in a fashion brand, often just because it has become commonplace by attracting too many new customers, the respective company regularly comes into trouble. This frequently happens to the younger brands but happens from time to time to brands for a more adult clientele too.

I do not want to conceal that brands indirectly also build cost advantages relative to rivals due to the earlier-explained scale effect. Establishing and sustaining a meaningful brand most often requires considerable fixed spending for personnel, advertising agencies, broadcasting time, newspaper advertisements, and so on. Due to this, size in revenues supports the position of a working brand as all these (fixed) marketing costs can be allocated over more sales units.

Assuming a good and strong product has already developed a respective powerful brand, the scale effect can bring the whole thing to even higher levels. A good marketing process can result in significant and constant cost advantages from the scale of the top line compared to the rivals, giving the competitive advantage due to the brand an additional fortification.

Even if smaller rivals can spend the same proportion of their revenues on product placement, sales force, advertising and the like as, for example, Apple or Nike do, they can't come close to matching these giants on absolute money deployed in order to attract new customers and to cultivate the existing customer base. The bigger players need to spend less in relative terms but achieve far more benefits from their marketing activities. A nation-wide or even international advertising campaign costs a huge and almost fixed amount of money that can be afforded only by the truly big firms. But although the spending is fixed, it results in an unlimited and unrivalled reach, giving the dominant players a unique opportunity to position themselves in the customers' heads and hearts. The brand strengthens over time as the dominant incumbents can constantly spend more on winning new generations of customers and developing long-term, emotion-based relationships with them. Via that, economies of scale in the marketing process perpetuate and amplify the advantageous position of the respective firms, which originally stems from great products, related brands, and customer loyalty.

Nevertheless, please keep in mind that marketing calls in the first place for management talent, not money. Or, differently put, also a mammoth marketing budget can be wasted without a sustaining effect if not wisely (i.e., constructively) spent.

The bottom line of this section is that brands can create a strong and durable competitive advantage for a firm towards its customers, but the popularity of a brand matters much less than its actual effect on the consumers' behaviour. If final users are willing to pay more for a product or are purchasing it with reliable regularity - solely because of the brand - you have compelling evidence for a competitive advantage. That is where the rubber meets the road. The investor has to check this economic effect of a brand carefully, as there are also plenty of well-known brands and related companies that struggle to earn sustainable returns. What counts is brand power, not brand awareness.

Keep in mind as well that brands are based on real products or services and attached customer values - not the other way round. A brilliant management has to come up with a compelling product or service and, subsequently, with a fitting marketing strategy. All this foremost calls for igniting ideas and also costs money, time, and persistent strategic effort. A well-run, scalable marketing process can then, when the overall business strategy is functioning, additionally result in cost advantages compared to peers, which enhance the bargaining position of the respective firm even further on the overall competitive ground.

Concerning risks, please memorize that a brand and the related reputation of a company are fragile constructs. In the optimal state, a firm's product or service is special in the customers' eyes, and the brand is in sync with the underlying value proposition. But what took a lot of management input, time, and money to build can be wrecked in just one scandal; in the worst case, the demolition of a brand's power is caused by the firm's own management.

Apart from this, a brand can suffer from overexpansion. Putting the same logotype or another recognition feature of a firm's value proposition on too many and too different products or services can dilute and hence weaken the core of a brand. The brand likely loses its meaning for the key customer base and, simultaneously, its pull.

Lastly, customers' tastes and perceptions can change over time due to external reasons that are not in control of an undertaking with a working brand. In consequence, the attractiveness of that brand for the customers can decrease and, in parallel, so can its economic value for the owning company. Due to all that, the investor must constantly have an eye on the dynamic relation between a certain brand, the underlying value proposition, and the customers that are attracted by all that.

Network Effect

In life, it generally matters what you know, but even more important is, whom you know. You might know people who create huge contact networks that make them desirable acquaintances because the more people they know, the more people they can connect with for mutual benefit. Their social value multiplies as the number of people in their networks grows.

Businesses that profit from the network effect are very similar; that is, the value of their product or service escalates with the number of customers.

The network effect is actually a sub-type or a positive form of switching costs. Customers also get sticky to a certain firm, but this time they do so because the benefit for them grows with each additional customer or user of the service or product. Both the company and its customers profit and gain value as the respective network expands.

This may appear to be pretty simple and common, but it is in reality fairly tricky and unusual. Think about your favourite restaurant. That business very likely crafts value for you by providing mouth-watering food and a good time at a reasonable and affordable price. But no matter how recommendable the restaurant is in your eyes, with too many people around, it can quickly become overcrowded and uncomfortable. The reason lies in the nature of the thing – **rivalry in consume**.

Retailers, manufacturers, banks – it is all the same story. Customers do rival for consume and at some point, it becomes a negative experience for them. These businesses benefit sure enough from a higher sales base, but you do not interact with them just because other people do as well; your motivation is different in each case, which stems likely from price, quality, or service level.

Now think about a credit card business like American Express. The rewards and perks that American Express offers its users help it to contend with other credit card firms, but if its cards were not accepted at millions of places where people want to spend money, American Express could offer triple the volume of sweeteners and would still have only a tiny number of paying customers. It is the colossal network of merchants that gives American Express its superior position in its game. The more places exist where you can really use your American Express card, the more valuable that card becomes to you as a client as well, which is the big reason behind every credit card company's continuous approach to get its particular payment system accepted at literally any little grocery shop or remote gas station.

There are actually only four large credit card networks, all rooted in the United States of America. These top four – Visa, MasterCard, American Express, and Discover – account for around 85 percent of all spending on credit cards in their home market. That represents a huge amount of market concentration, and it illustrates that the network effect can be extremely forceful as it tends to create natural monopolies and oligopolies.[61]

If the value of a product or service rises with the number of people using it, the most valuable will be the ones that persuade the vast majority of users, creating an upward spiral that ousts smaller networks (if they even exist) and amplifies the size of the dominant network. And as the dominant network gets bigger, it intensifies its attractiveness. With each additional user or customer, the customer loyalty strengthens all the more, making the market leader more powerful.

Interestingly, growth in size and strength do not go hand in hand. The benefit for a firm from having a larger network is non-linear, which means that the economic value of the network expands at a faster rate than its absolute size.

But although the network effect tends to form concentrated markets, it is only fair to mention that not every concentrated market structure stems from it. Other effects can also trigger a propensity to

---

[61] Pat Dorsey, *The Little Book that Builds Wealth: The Knockout Formula for Finding Great Investments* (Hoboken, New Jersey: John Wiley & Sons, 2008).

concentrate around a market leader. Due to its very nature, there are not many businesses that can benefit from the network effect.

As described, the network effect initially comes from a strategic decision to set up or enter a certain business and to bring it to a certain size, but its vast power is mainly derived from the structure of the business and the nature of the customer value. From a certain customer base or critical mass onward, the network effect structurally serves the firm, gradually building up the power of attraction with every additional client.

The strategic imperative, hence, is clear: a firm that wants to experience the network effect must be (one of) the first within the respective business, actively growing its customer base at least to the chief hurdle or tipping point from where the structurally functioning network effect begins to kick in. If it comes to the competitive advantage from networks, in most instances the winner truly takes it all. Due to that, the right start and rapid expansion of the business in its early stages is of the highest priority, not only for the company's overall success, but for its economic viability.

Another globally represented company that also obtains a good portion of its negotiation power towards the customer side from the network effect is Microsoft. Lots of people use its software products Microsoft Office Word or Excel. It is hard to argue that Microsoft Windows is the acme of PC operating systems, but its massive user base means that you as an individual definitely have to know how to operate a Windows-based PC in order to stand your ground in the business world of today. Even if a rival or substitute showed up on the scene next week with a writing processor or a spreadsheet calculator program that was way easier to use and half the price, it would have a hard time gaining a meaning in the market because Microsoft's Word and Excel, as they were more or less the first, are the common language of knowledge workers around the globe. The users would likely be resistant to learning the new programs, and even more critical, would have to worry if they can share their information with other users outside the accustomed system.[62]

As you might have noticed, American Express and Microsoft have one thing in common regarding their business models and the respective customer values – information. In general, the network effect occurs a good deal more amongst businesses based on information sharing, knowledge transfer, or connecting users rather than amongst businesses based on physical products or labour-intense services.

This has two distinct reasons: one is attached to the supply side, one to the demand side of a business.

Starting with the supply side, it is mostly knowledge or information-based and hence highly scalable business models that can have the network effect. Neither the company nor its products or services have strict physical boundaries. Due to that, the supply side is able to generate value for additional customers at virtually no incremental costs. If the business model were not highly scalable, the supply

---

[62] Pat Dorsey, *The Little Book that Builds Wealth: The Knockout Formula for Finding Great Investments* (Hoboken, New Jersey: John Wiley & Sons, 2008).

side would restrict an accretive customer base, a key element of the network effect.

Looking at the demand side, the network effect is rooted in what we economists call **non-rival goods**. For instance, all customers of American Express can use the credit card system simultaneously and hassle-free. And no person's use of Microsoft software impedes the ability of others to apply it at the same time. In stark contrast, most physical products can be used by only one person at a time – no one can eat the meal I am eating or use the cell phone I am using in that same moment. Due to the rivalry in consumption, such things are labelled **rival goods**.[63]

But for the creation of a real network effect, the value of the product or service for the customer side must clearly rise with every additional customer. So it is not enough if the value for each customer or user is independent from the general customer base. Every single customer or user must clearly benefit from a growing demand for the respective product or service.

As an investor, you need to unambiguously ascertain if an increase in size and density of a network generates more value not only for the company but also for each customer – this is in fact the ultimate check for a network effect. Then, and only then, the network effect leads to a valuable win-win situation for both the possessing firm and its customers.

---

[63] Food represents a class of non-durable, rival goods; it ceases to exist after consumption. A cell phone, in contrast, belongs to the group of durable, rival goods; other individuals may use it, but only after the current user is finished.

Facebook, a very popular online social networking service provider in these days, and eBay, the legendary e-commerce platform, are two other companies that owe much of their prosperousness to the network effect.

To sum up, the initiation of a network effect is a lot easier said than done. Besides some structural preconditions to be met, management needs to put its focus especially on the start-up phase. There is no real second place in this game. But once up and running, the network effect gives the respective, fortunate firm a powerful, because structural, competitive advantage towards its customers.

Apart from that, you can say that the network effect works in some way as an economic moat towards potential rivals too. A newcomer in such market would have to replicate the entire network – or at least would have to come close to it – before users would see more value in the new network and switch away from the old-established one. Openly speaking, that is really a tall order. It can happen under some very special circumstances, but network-based businesses are usually pretty durable due to the elaborated, structural reasons.

Notwithstanding its power, the network effect can of course also weaken or vanish if a formerly locked network opens up, either due to a structural change of the underlying customer need / demand or due to an innovative strategy from somebody else, offering the same customer value in a fresh and superior way. So even if the network effect is functioning and powerful, there is always a risk that structural changes on the demand side or a strategic action from the beloved external rivalry can destroy its value.

Consequently, the investor needs to be on the watch for general trends in consumers' demand and offered solutions by other parties; these are the main areas of risk for an investor regarding an existing network effect.

V. The Valuation

Price Is What You Pay, Value Is What You Get

Why do we have to value stocks? We defined and maybe identified already a wonderful business – why not just rush and grab some stocks? The explanation was already mentioned before: a proper valuation increases your chances for a good investment return and decreases your investment risk at the same time.

In the end, value from your viewpoint as the shareholder (i.e., investor) is an adequate, positive net cash flow to you, building a difference between the cash you pay for a company's stock and the cash you get out of your investment in return.

When buying a stock, you acquire a part of a company's book equity at a premium. With valuation, you challenge the current market price for a stock, so the book value of the equity as well as the premium for it.

The stock price should reflect the shareholder value, which in turn is based on some already known value drivers: the strength of the existing customer need / demand, the quality of the firm's value proposition and the relating business model, the overall risk of the business, the competitive advantages, and the growth prospects. It is all of them that drive value and, in the long run, share prices. Unfortunately, as all these drivers cumulate in one figure, the share price, it is almost impossible to

The Valuation

separate a single one.

Nevertheless, by having a good understanding about the customer need / demand, the value proposition, the business model, the competitive advantages, and the magnitude and likelihood of the overall risks, these basic elements become rationally assessable to you. What is only left, then, are the growth prospects, for which you should not pay too much either.

So very frankly, valuation is not a precise concept, and value is not one universal figure. Every investor has a specific approach and an individual idea about return and risk when seeking investments. And as everybody is different, value differs from each single investor's angle. Thus, valuation always gives you only a reasonable but subjective reference point, reflecting your personal expectations regarding cash flows, risk, and return.

Consequently, value is your view on a company, which you compare with the current stock price in order to challenge the market. Value in this regard can be linked to a buying price you have to wait for in order to satisfy your personal appetite for risk and return. And no matter how wonderful a business might be, at certain levels the respective stocks get too pricey. Your appetite for return and risk will just not be satisfied if you pay too much for what you get. A too-steep purchase price will lessen your overall investment return and elevate your investment risk. To avoid that, valuation is a vital part of my investment approach.

It may sound again trivial to you, but the first and foremost goal is not to lose money and hence to get your invested capital back as soon and safe as possible. Any additional, positive net cash flow out of the stock investment comes as a surplus and hopefully fulfils your overall return expectations in the end. Please keep this simple but essential rule in mind when thinking about any stock investment going forward.

In order to achieve a reasonable buy, valuation needs to be structured as a two-step process: understanding value is the first step, and estimating value is the second step.

The Valuation

Step One: Understanding Value

Companies create value for their owners by investing cash today in order to generate more cash in the future. The amount of value made is the difference between money spent and cash inflows from that – adjusted for the fact that tomorrow's cash flows are worth less than today's. In addition to that, each business has a specific risk / return pattern that triggers particular funding costs for the respective firm.

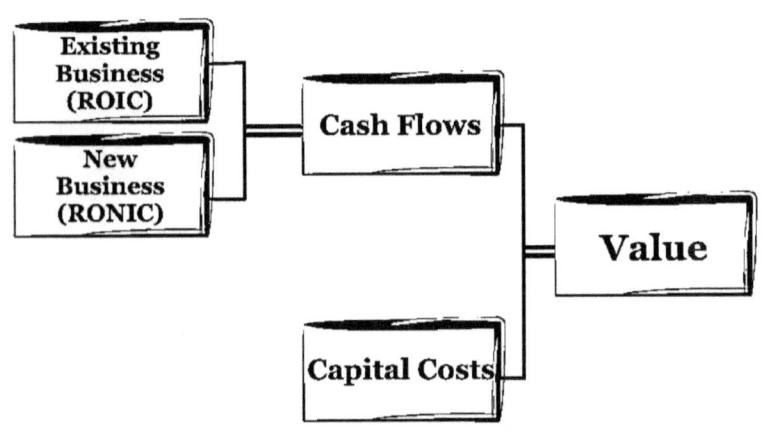

Exhibit 5.1 **The Concept of Value**

One might expect a kind of universal agreement on how to measure and manage the value of a firm, but this is not the case. Many executives, boards, and even analysts still almost obsessively focus on net earnings and net earnings growth. But although net earnings and net earnings growth are usually also positively correlated with cash flows, they do not tell the real story of value creation, and focusing on these financial measures often leads the company astray.

Yes, in the end, shareholder return is also much about net earnings and net earnings growth, but they alone just do not reflect the vital role of margins and capital utilisation, expressed by the ROIC ratio.[64] The ROIC represents a firm's pricing power and sales volume, (operating) cost structure, and, last but not least, (operating) asset investment requirements in order to generate the customer value and to compete in the capitalistic game. The ROIC embodies with EBIT or NOPAT in the nominator and operating assets in the denominator the two true factors that reflect the drivers for value – **operating profit margin** and **asset turnover**.

A company's ROIC determines and expresses how its revenues get converted into cash inflows. Revenues are the ultimate source for cash inflows and a direct mirroring of the firm's customer value as well as its ultimate competitive position. And ROIC's two inherent factors, operating profit margin and asset turnover, are both about the revenues. What is required in terms of regular (operating) costs to earn them? And what investments in (operating) assets are needed to generate them? In both value factors, operating profit margin and asset turnover, revenues play the central role.

---

[64] Tim Koller, Richard Dobbs, and Bill Huyett, *Value: The Four Cornerstones of Corporate Finance* (Hoboken, New Jersey: John Wiley & Sons, 2011).

All in all, ROIC is the financial manifestation of the firm's value proposition and related business model, risks, competitive advantages, and growth opportunities; every value driver finally finds its expression in ROIC.

A company's management that is aware of the ROIC concept can detect, communicate, and actively drive value. Therefore, a firm's value is ultimately measured and managed best with the ROIC concept. As the centre of value creation, ROIC with its inherent components deserves the highest attention from the firm's management and the investor.

As you see above in the graph, the value of a company can be segregated further into two areas: existing (i.e., ongoing) business and new business in the form of additional revenue streams, each with its own economics.

While so-called "value investors" tend to primarily look at the value of the ongoing business, "growth investors" put more emphasis on future opportunities, or the new business. Indeed, growth can be an additional source of value. But as new business can come in many forms, each with its own specifics and resulting profitability,[65] a prudent investor must be careful while thoroughly understanding and pricing it.

---

[65] ***Return on new invested capital*** (***RONIC***) represents the incremental ROIC of new business (i.e., of growth in revenues).

Existing Business

A common misperception in the financial community is to think that a company grows at the expansion rates of its revenues or net earnings. Yes, new business is one of the sources from which value (i.e., net cash flows) for a company can come. But a company, its total cash flows, and the consequential value do not grow at that rate.

In its steady state, a firm's value thrives and prospers with the percentage at which the revenues are turned into cash, expressed by the ROIC applying to the (total) existing business. The respective (total) cash flow is then used by the management to fund daily operations, do investments, or pay money to the shareholders and banks of the company.[66]

Another common misconception out there is that financial leverage actively drives value - something I will tackle in more detail a little bit later. Apart from this, many investors care too much about the firm's taxes and tax rates. Granted, tax efficiency keeps money in the firm and hence should be on the management's agenda but taxes, like financing, are no viable sources of cash flows to the firm. Management actions like negotiating with banks or arguing with tax authorities economise money but do not generate it in the first place. Ultimately, it is the operating business that intrinsically makes cash and hence value.

---

[66] ROIC is the maximum (intrinsic) growth rate of a company's assets if no dividends are paid or share repurchases are made (i.e., if the retention rate, aka reinvestment ratio, is 100 percent).

The Valuation

A breakdown of return on equity (ROE),[67] a financial measure for the rate of return for the firm's shareholders, gives you the overview of which factors really represent value:[68]

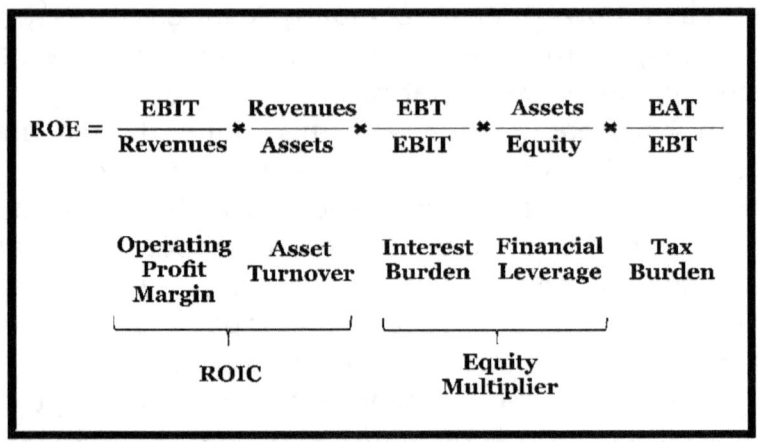

Exhibit 5.2 **The Dupont - Equation**

In the core, it is the operating profit margin as well as the asset turnover of a firm where sustainable value in the form of cash flows can come from. Therefore, these two financial ratios should be in the centre of

---

[67] **Return on equity** is defined as the EAT (aka net result) divided by the (average) shareholder's equity. ROE is a pivotal profitability ratio that measures the ability of a firm to generate (accounting) profits from its shareholders' equity stakes. Compared to ROIC, ROE is additionally influenced and driven by the financial leverage of the company.

[68] The **Dupont-Analysis** (aka **Dupont-Equation**) is a mathematical expression which breaks the ROE ratio down into five parts. The name comes from the DuPont Corporation, that started using this formula in the 1920s. As you can see in the formula, ROIC is actually the ROE of a company that is completely financed with equity; the equity multiplier equals one then.

your analysis in order to get deeper into the firm's value creation process.

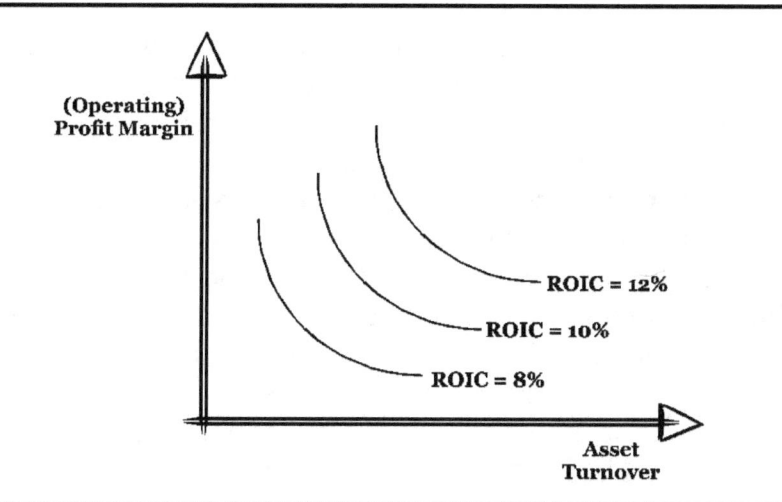

Exhibit 5.3 ROIC - Isoquants

Operating Profit Margin

Through dividing each type of operational cost by total revenues, you get an idea what it takes from a cost perspective in relative terms to earn one unit of such revenues. In addition, you can actually detect which distinct input factors are required to create a particular customer value, for example, labour force or raw materials like oil, copper, woods, or sugar. Also, the investment costs or the use of machines become visible in a profit margin in the form of depreciation and amortization.

All in all, by scrutinising the cost structure in relative terms, you get not only an indication of the company's profitability with regard to the revenues and the related operating costs but also a deeper understanding about how the company works and where competitive advantages could rest.

A high and stable profit margin can be in general the expression of pricing power due to a favourable position of the respective firm on the competitive field. But operational efficiency in the process landscape and economies of scale, if fixed costs apply, can also boost profit margins.

To find the true reason, an investor would need to have further information regarding pricing, operational developments, and the fundamental cost structure. Company presentations as well as more independent sources like audit reports can be of practical help for an investor in this regard.

The more flexible (i.e., variable) the operating cost structure of a business is, the higher its **cost adaptability**, resulting in less risk for the undertaking itself as well as the investors. In such cases, the revenues do not need to expose predictability and a kind of stiffness in order to safeguard the firm's profitability. Instead, the firm's operating cost structure can be quickly adjusted in case revenues drop for some unforeseen, external reason.

So cost adaptability and the related flexibility (i.e., variability) of the operating cost structure are definitely good things to have, especially from a risk perspective. But fixed costs are not per se "bad". Actually, the question if fixed costs are positive or negative for a firm depends on the reason for the incurring fixed costs and their effect on the top line. As I explained earlier, many competitive advantages stem from operating processes, which in turn structurally create a certain level of fixed costs. With that, operating processes and related competitive advantages can add for sure some inflexibility to a firm's operating cost structure, but they also aid the respective businesses to preserve the quantity and quality of their revenues even in times of economic downs. Negotiated long-term contracts, for example, in the optimum with certain price-escalation clauses and take-or-pay elements, guarantee a fixed revenue stream over a certain, stipulated space of time. With such favourable terms and conditions in place, a firm's revenue levels stay constant and strong even through recessionary times, resulting in corresponding profit margins. Therefore, the key question regarding fixed costs is what kind of operating processes, related competitive advantages (i.e., negotiation power) and revenues are effectuated with them.

As a minimum requirement, a wonderful business should be able to gently pass its own inflation of costs to the customers on a regular basis.

Summing up, it is either a very flexible (i.e., quite variable) operating cost structure we want to see as investors or a stiffer (i.e., more fixed) operating cost structure and corresponding competitive advantages, which then result in adequate and pre-visible (i.e., safe) revenues.

Operational excellence and process management have, of course, a weighty impact on profit margins too. Doing the right things in the right ways pays off in spades. Efficacious efforts aimed to expedite efficiency and productivity can be directly seen in the income statement and related profit margins. But also signs of quality like safety, reliability, and sustainability can become visible in an income statement. In point of fact, by not having positions for environmental damages, warranty costs, or legal charges in its financial books over longer periods of time, a company somehow proves that it is in an easy business and / or that it follows safe, reliable, and sustainable procedures.

Apart from all this, exchange rates between different currencies can impact profit margins. If, for instance, revenues are made in foreign currency, but production costs accrue in the domestic currency, an appreciation of the foreign currency would definitely have a positive effect on a firm's bottom line. This holds true especially if the price is a major argument in the customers' buying decisions. However and needless to say, this can go the other way around too. An investor ought to be cognisant of this macro-economic aspect, although there are not too many measures against it. From an investor's perspective, apart from waiving an investment in such cases, a well-diversified portfolio will be the most effective way to mitigate adverse currency developments in single companies (i.e., single stock positions).

Asset Turnover

The asset turnover ratio of a company includes revenues too - this time in the nominator. And with the (operating) assets in the denominator, this ratio can also tell you how efficiently or productively the company creates its customer value and how well it generally competes with all the different economic players. Efficiency and productivity in turn relate again to the big topic of operational excellence, which, as you can see, shows up not only in the profit-and-loss statement in the form of operating costs and operating profit margins but also at the asset side of a firm's balance sheet. When it comes to the balance sheet, the major, value-driving subject is efficient or productive asset (i.e., capital) utilisation.

All in all, a company has to invest money and to use some types of assets in order to create its customer value. Fixed tangible as well as intangible assets and working capital items such as inventory, trade receivables, and a decent level of cash to fund the day-to-day operations are part of the balance sheets of almost all companies.

Looking at these assets from an industry level, you will often find several similarities, as the respective customer value of that industry is naturally requiring a certain set of assets. Nevertheless, the additional and unique appliance of available technology and a good management strategy can definitely make a difference between peers, although companies might operate for the most part with the same kind of assets.

It's worthwhile to mention that the firm's direct negotiation power towards its customers and suppliers also impacts asset levels and, with that, a firm's asset turnover ratio.

To start with, the working capital of a firm and related financial ratios can provide you with plenty of indications and evidence about two crucial underlying aspects of a wonderful business – namely, operational excellence and negotiation power (i.e., competitive advantages).

Take **net working capital to revenues** as a variation of the asset turnover ratio, for instance. While stable or even rising revenue levels will mainly stem from good demand and competitive advantages at work, proper management speeds up a firm's cash conversion cycle and supports efficient working capital levels. Outsourcing of functions, lean production, just-in-time delivery, factoring, or cash pooling – in the end, all these management tools and actions are intended to configure the operating asset base as efficiently and productively as possible.

But, yes, balance sheet positions like inventories, trade receivables, and trade liabilities are influenced by the negotiation power in the capitalistic game too. By having a good position to drive the bargains, a firm can ask both groups, the customers as well as the suppliers, for better terms and conditions, resulting in lower levels of working capital in the balance sheet and an improved asset turnover ratio.

To carve out more clearly the aspect of negotiation power, the ratio of **trade receivables to trade liabilities** is in fact a pretty good indicator for the bargaining position of an incumbent firm towards its customers on the one hand and its suppliers on the other hand.

It is more the development of this balance sheet ratio over time that flags whether the company's standpoint directly along the value chain actually improves, deteriorates, or just remains constant.

Trade receivables tend to be lower on average if

the position to bargain towards customers is high.[69] In the end, trade receivables represent regularly an interest-free loan to the customers, and having low levels saves a company real money here. A current liability position that can tell you something about a firm's bargaining position is primarily trade payables to suppliers. Here, a firm is actually taking a kind of interest-free loan from its suppliers. The bigger the outstanding amounts are and the longer the suppliers have to wait for the due money, the better the owing firm's financials.

So getting paid as soon as possible and postponing the settlement of own outstanding amounts as far as possible into the future helps a firm to improve its profitability but depends largely on its negotiation power along the value chain.

Days sales outstanding (DSO)[70] - This ratio can tell you something about an incumbent firm's negotiation power towards its customers, but besides this, it can also give you a hint about the general customer quality (i.e., customer solvency) of a business.

---

[69] Taking the assumption that management tools and actions like factoring are the same over the analysed space of time. High levels of trade receivables in turn do not necessarily stem only from a weak bargaining angle of a firm towards its customers; it can also be that the customers have problems with their liquidity. To avoid misinterpretations, the solvency of a firm's customers has to be separately checked (e.g., with the DSO ratio).

[70] DSO ratio equals trade receivables divided by average sales per day or, alternatively, trade receivables divided by (annual sales divided by 365 days). Of course, seasonal patterns can apply as well. DSO can vary from month to month and over the course of a year with a company's seasonal business cycle without any change in the firm's bargaining position or the customer solvency in general.

The Valuation

It should not necessarily be your first thought, but the DSO ratio should be checked in order to prevent negative surprises from your investment in the form of low-quality (i.e., non-performing) trade receivables. It goes without saying: solvent and reliable customers are a mandatory, structural element of a wonderful business, and you should try to collect conclusive evidence if that is really the case.

Let us turn now to the tangible fixed assets of an undertaking. The asset intensity can be lowered with regard to fixed tangibles too. Good planning and crisp execution, but even more a good negotiation position towards the suppliers, can significantly reduce the capital expenditure needs for the respective firm, finally resulting in a higher (i.e., better) asset turnover ratio.

The ratio of **capital expenditures to depreciation** shows you in the first place if a company grows or shrinks its asset base over time. But only taking the development of this ratio again in relation to the development of the revenues will give you the gist. Especially if the asset base rises and revenues stay flat or even shrink in the same period of time, an investor should urgently search for the exact reasons.

In the worst case, such a scenario could come from a vaguely defined, badly conducted investment process or just inefficient asset management. Big investments only in order to maintain the existing fixed asset base or a deteriorating purchasing power towards suppliers are further bad reasons.

In the best case, however, it is simply a major ramp up in new business before the respective project or assets start producing fresh revenues.

The ratio of **capital expenditures to revenues** would head you in the same direction, delivering insights into how much money needs to be invested in order to generate one unit of revenues. While a deteriorating ratio can indicate that capital expenditures are mainly spent on unpretentious maintenance or the other, negative reasons mentioned before, a prospering ratio can indicate higher operational excellence or lucrative investments in new growth opportunities via additional capacity or innovation.

But watch it – just separating capital expenditures into "growth" and "maintenance" is firstly not easy and secondly often too short. Yes, capital expenditures for growth are a good thing for value - if the related incremental ROIC is appropriate.

Nevertheless, money can also be profitably spent without touching top line. Investments in safety standards and procedures are mandatory not only to protect lives and the environment within the ongoing business activities but also to safeguard and optimise further growth.

Besides this, although improvements of efficiency and productivity in the value creation process cost money in the beginning, these capital expenditures enable a company to get the most excellence out of its current operations. Amounts spent that way do not directly result in more business. But that does not mean that they are of no value for the company. They can add value - just indirectly.

As an investor, you are therefore asked to deeply dig into the investment budget of a company; only this way can you obtain an all-embracing view and proper judgement about a company's capital budget and its impact on (long-term) profitability and value.

Aside from the above, please see that a good or even wonderful business model does not per se have to be "capital-light".[71] Again, all depends on the corresponding revenues.

If the revenues get fixed (i.e., negotiated) with the customer ex ante, before the assets are bought (i.e., the investments are made), capital-intensive businesses can be wonderful as well. Assuming a firm's negotiation position is powerful enough, such sureness in the top line can be facilitated, for instance, through long-term contracts with or other strong commitments from the customer side. Ideally, both components of the revenues, prices[72] and volumes[73], get stipulated with the clientele in a dependable manner.

The returns under such circumstances are predictable (i.e., reasonably certain) and the risk of unintended overcapacities or unprofitable investments is tamed somewhat.[74]

---

[71] Aka "asset-light". A "capital-light" business does not require huge amounts of assets in the balance sheet (i.e., capital investments) in relation to the revenues made.

[72] For example, by means of negotiated price lists or commonly agreed cost plus approaches.

[73] For example, by means of predetermined minimum purchase quantities or guarantees about certain degrees of capacity utilisation.

[74] Please also note that, in many cases, the source of a competitive advantage is a physical (i.e., tangible) asset that needs to be in the firm's balance sheet and the denominator of ROIC, respectively. Hence, although capital-intensive, such business can indeed be wonderful. As described - in the end, it is all about the quality of the relating revenues.

Lastly, currency effects also play a role in the asset turnover ratio, just like in the operating profit margin ratio. If assets are denominated in foreign currencies, movements in the exchange rates can especially impact the values of current assets. If, for example, the value of some current assets gets pumped up in the course of a foreign currency appreciation, the asset turnover ratio will slow down and impact the overall ROIC in a negative way.

Because the effect from currency exchange rates on ROIC via the asset turnover effects can be quite substantial, an investor should definitely bear that angle in mind when analysing a company.

Financial Leverage – Driving Shareholders' Return and Risk, Not Value!

Debt financing is the direct link between ROIC and ROE. But although ROE, like ROIC, is such a central capital return ratio, the **equity multiplier** in it does really not contribute to a company's total value. ROIC determines and shows how a firm's revenues are converted into value-adding net cash flows; ROE measures how the shareholders' capital actually benefits and grows.

By changing a firm's level of debt financing, leadership can actively accelerate or tame the return and risk for its shareholders. By adding more bank loans, for instance, to the balance sheet, the more expensive equity will get substituted and the net result decreases due to higher interest expenses. Actually, both the shareholder's equity in the denominator and net result in the nominator of ROE decrease when debt levels are ascending. But as the denominator effect predominates, ROE can be geared up just via enhanced debt levels. Also due to the different treatment of equity and debt from a tax standpoint, the use of debt for running a company makes sense. At some degree of financial leverage, though, the benefits from the tax deductibility of interest expenses and the substitution of "expensive" equity with "cheap" bank loans get balanced out and then get even overcompensated by the rising costs due to the risks of financial distress and bankruptcy. As bank loans and related interests are normally senior to equity and related dividends, outstanding financial debt and interest payables have always to be acquitted first. So an increased level of bank loans in the balance sheet enhances not only the return for the shareholders via the **financial leverage effect** and the **tax shield** from debt financing, it also intensifies their risk position through more fixed costs, contractual obligations (i.e., higher dependence on banks) and, subsequently, an elevated possibility of bankruptcy in economically bad times. Financial leverage constitutes a trade-off between risk and return for the company as well as its shareholders.

With that, debt financing is in truth a kind of double-edged sword. The financial leverage effect gears the ROE up in any direction. Financial leveraging simply reallocates the total return and risk between the different providers of capital, classically shareholders and banks. The amplified return to the shareholders is therefore not for free; it comes at additional costs for them – in the form of additional risk. In essence, the financial leverage of a company has nothing to do with value creation for the total firm but has to do with leveraging return as well as risk for the shareholders at the same time.

So once again, the value of an undertaking is generally generated at the left side of the balance sheet. The assets of a company, not the capital obligations, earn the money.

Consequently, the management should not overcook the meaning of an exact and "optimal" point for debt financing for the overall success of the company. Instead, the management should seek reliable, cost efficient, and flexible financing sources while keeping debt levels within a healthy band from the particular business perspective.

(Shareholder's) **equity to total assets** and (financial) **gearing**[75] are balanced sheet-based debt financing ratios. Appropriate levels for such ratios depend mainly on the degrees of liquidity as well as the quality of the firm's assets, functioning as securities for the banks or other lenders.

Earnings-related ratios like **net debt to EBITDA** can also help a company's management to strike the right balance between return and risk for the shareholders. The EBITDA in the financing relation serves as a proxy for operating cash flow before changes in the operating assets and represents the firm's basic ability to serve its financial obligations from ongoing business activities.

---

[75] (Net) debt divided by shareholder's equity, with net debt as financial debt minus cash balance.

The Valuation

All in all, financial leverage is not a driver for value. However, debt financing can be the source of additional return for existing shareholders if the financial condition of the respective firm is robust and stable. As financial leverage is definitely also a source of risk for a company and its shareholders, especially in dire economic straits, the management should steer debt financing to levels that best suit the overall business, the firm's average earnings power, and the nature of its assets.

Also from a potentially new investor's angle, a firm's financial leverage should be appropriate in relation to its earnings power and the quality of its balance sheet, but most importantly, better lower than higher. Financial health and solvency will help a company to survive in economic downturns, subsequently lowering the risk for newly entering investors too. In addition to that, financial flexibility enables a company to catch hold of a promising occasion the moment it shows up, which in turn enhances the attractiveness of such undertaking from any investor's point of view.

Apart from checking if management puts such logics into practise, investors can interpret the financial leverage also as an indirect indication if a company is really in possession of a profitable and advantaged business.

If a firm is constantly leveraged to the maximum level of debt or is regularly in desperate need of fresh money from outside sources, it clearly does not embody a wonderful business.

New Business

As indicated already, new business can of course bring value to a company in the form of additional revenues and resulting net cash flows too. But although growth or new business is high on the agenda of many investors, it just complements the total picture. Many investors assume that all (revenue) growth earns the same ROIC and hence generates the same value – but this is not realistic.

The growth of revenues is undeniably a good part of a firm's total value, but each type of growth or set of additional revenues comes with its specific profitability or incremental ROIC (i.e., RONIC) and therefore creates its unique amount of value.

For example, growth from creating completely new product categories tends to create more value than growth from pricing and promotion tactics in order to gain market share from peers.

Just as management and investors need to understand whether certain core strategies will lead to high and sustainable ROIC, they also must know which growth opportunities for a company will generate the highest value at the end.[76]

---

[76] Please keep in mind that good managers first and foremost invest in the creation, upgrade, or fortification of a company's competitive advantages and the resulting negotiation power. So no matter if the management hunts for completely new business lines and markets or tries to grow its core business, please satisfy yourself every time that the company's capital is wisely allocated to this indispensable element of a wonderful business.

The Valuation

In the main, there are five types of growth:[77]

1. Novel markets
2. Differentiated, value-added products / services
3. Price increases
4. Market share increase
5. Acquisitions

Organic growth via completely new markets typically creates the most value for shareholders in relation to the other types, while acquisitions (i.e., inorganic growth) typically create the least, if any. Differentiated and value-added products or services in order to attract more or new kinds of customers, price increases, and market share expansion in an existing market also represent organic growth and rank in the middle with regard to economic attractiveness.

See that each of the major growth types can be further broken down into subtypes; for instance, you can increase market share by either lowering prices or improving efforts to market and sell your product or service. Additionally, the competitive structure and behaviour of an industry will affect the value created from each type of growth. So the variations of growth types and their value impact can be enormous.

A useful way to assess the potential for value creation from a particular type of growth is to study which economic party loses when a company grows its revenues and how the loser can and likely will

---

[77] Patrick Viguerie, Sven Smit, and Mehrdad Baghai, *The Granularity of Growth: How to Identify the Sources of Growth and Drive Enduring Company Performance* (Hoboken, New Jersey: John Wiley & Sons, 2008).

respond or retaliate.[78]

For instance, attempts to increase the market share through price competition come at the expense of direct rivals. But if those opponents are strong enough to retaliate or even hang on for the duration of the price war, the growth associated with the increased market share probably will not create much value. If price discounting becomes the norm, this may even reduce the firm's value.

Similarly, price raises will not create much value for the respective firm unless customers have a tough time to switch to peers, to reduce their consumption, or to find substitutes.

At the very top in the domain of profitable growth are early, fast-growing markets that take revenues from distant industries, not from immediate rivals. Such markets usually entail some form of ground-breaking technology that leads to entirely new product or service categories. For example, the smartphone and related apps satisfied a totally new customer demand when that invention came out. Traditional mobile phones could not retaliate, as they could just not offer the same value proposition. With that, high growth in the underlying product market tends to create the most value of all growth categories because it typically comes at the expense of companies in other industries, which sometimes do not even know to whom they are losing ground. Such unaware companies have, in this case, the least ability to get even.

In the best case, the company that received a

---

[78] Robert E. Hoskisson, Michael A. Hitt, and R. Duane Ireland, *Competing for Advantage* (Mason, Ohio: Thomson South-Western, 2004).

positive feedback from the demand side concerning its innovative product or service enjoys on top legal protection from plagiarism via a patent or the like. With such an economic moat around its novel value proposition, the pioneering company remains unchallenged for some time and can collect its well-deserved proceeds in the meantime.

The second-highest value creation comes from getting current customers to buy more of a value-added product or a modification of it.

As an example, if Procter & Gamble convinces customers to wash their hands more frequently or to use a soap with a new fragrance or colour, the market for hand soap will pick up – and direct rivals will not retaliate because they benefit as well. The ROIC associated with these additional revenues is likely to be high because the manufacturing and distribution systems can typically absorb the additional sales at little additional cost; in other words, the company benefits from economies of scale and scope.

But if the scalability of the business is low due to its very nature or management inefficiencies, the benefit might not be worth mentioning as the accelerating incremental costs for the additional business would just erase profitability.

Such growth strategies based on product differentiation and development of value-added products, motivating current customers to buy more, or attracting new customers, can mostly be observed in end consumer industries. There, they frequently result in the highest returns on capital because such plans do not require heavy, new investments; companies can add further product variations to their existing factory lines and distribution systems. Moreover, the investments required for value-added / differentiated products are doled out over time; if the preliminary results are not promising, the respective funding can be scaled back or cancelled. Having said that, it should also be noted that this type of growth does not come without any risk either. It needs ideas, money for R&D, marketing (i.e., investments in existing brands), and often many tries to become successful in a market with a product variation. Nonetheless, attracting new customers with differentiated / value-added products to a somehow already existing market can create substantial value.

To give you an example, consumer packaged goods companies, such as Unilever with "Axe" as one of its brands and Johnson & Johnson with its "Neutrogena Men" brand, increased the growth of their skin care products by convincing men to use them.[79] Once again, rivals did not retaliate because they also experienced higher growth from the overall trend. But men's skin care products are not that different from women's, so much of the costs from the R&D, manufacturing, and distribution processes could be shared with the already existing sales base. The major incremental costs mainly stem from increased marketing and advertising activities, which were in a healthy proportion to the additional revenues made.

---

[79] „Convincing", in this context, means to properly market a product in order to stress the benefits from using it. Ultimately, there has to be a need / demand from the customer side; no marketing can "create" a need and a resulting demand on a sustainable basis. The need / demand for men's cosmetics, for example, was driven by a structural change in modern society and the shifted social role of men.

The Valuation

Price increases represent, down the ladder, the next growth category. Although price increases create value, if the volume declines are minimal in the following, they normally tend to be not repeatable. Whether a company can raise prices depends anyway on its pricing power, driven by its particular negotiation power towards customers and its general bargaining position on the economic field. But even if a company or group of rivals gets away with an extra price raise this year, they are unlikely to get another increase in the next year as well. Further, the escalation this year could be eroded again in future years. If companies regularly inflated prices faster than their costs grew, you would observe sustainably climbing profit margins, which is a rare phenomenon in reality. Yet some few, wonderful companies out there are able to pass through their additional costs to the customer on a regular or even contractual basis.

The value created via market share expansion mainly depends on two things: the rate at which the underlying product grows and the way additional market share is gained.

For example, when a company enlarges its share through aggressive advertising in a rapidly growing market, rivals may still grow their absolute revenues at an attractive rate as well, so they may not retaliate.

Gaining share in a developed market, however, is more likely to result in heavy-duty retaliation by rivals. Especially in mature or concentrated markets, gaining share from rivals through pricing, promotion, or marketing rarely creates any value.

As Amazon continued expanding into the US

consumer electronics retail market in 2009, Walmart retaliated with price cuts on such key products as top-selling video games and game consoles, even though Amazon's sales were a fraction of Walmart's in the same year. As top line-size is the dominating success factor for retailers and the main source for a superior negotiation position in this industry, the reaction of the long-established, leading company was reasonable. Nevertheless, the example illustrates the common drawback of a purely volume-based or economies-of-scale strategy under such circumstances – it normally hurts all players, including the market leader too.

In effect, share battles in mature or concentrated markets often only cause a cycle of share wins and losses while the incumbent companies' profit margins get squeezed but rarely lead to a permanent share gain for one particular player - unless one player changes the product itself, or its delivery, substantially enough to effectively create a new value proposition. An exception is when share is gained from small, weak rivals who are entirely forced out of the market. Also, a takeover (i.e., inorganic growth) within the relevant market can mix up the old order but regularly comes at quite some price, as you will read a little bit later. Otherwise, every incumbent firm, especially the market leader, keeps its position in terms of volume size.[80]

---

[80] Tim Koller, Richard Dobbs, and Bill Huyett, *Value: The Four Cornerstones of Corporate Finance* (Hoboken, New Jersey: John Wiley & Sons, 2011).

The Valuation

Above all, the question about how profitable organic growth is for a company depends not only on the quality of the additional revenues and the underlying prices, volumes, and terms but also on the scalability of the business model.

Scalability is the capability of a system, network, or process to handle a growing amount of work without incremental costs. Apart from the normal accretion in consumption of raw materials (i.e., variable costs), such additional costs attributable to higher output levels can come not only from erratically higher needs for operating assets or personnel but also from an elevated complexity in the form of more organisational costs or waste of time. Scalability is largely inherent in the business model and hence structural in nature once operations have been commenced.

A **perfectly scalable** business has no incremental costs to bear at all – no variable costs, no complexities, no additional time spending, and no further requirements for (fixed) operating assets or additional personnel. Once all operating processes are set up, staffed with human capabilities, and equipped with the required assets, no incremental costs would accrue in the course of an enhanced business activity. When the sales base rises, profitability of such a business rockets because neither additional variable and fixed costs, nor complexities incur. The typical scale effect (i.e., a fixed-cost degression) kicks in to full extent.

However, please see again that scalability is not about low or zero fixed costs. Scalability applies in case the incremental costs rise at a (much) lower percentage than the corresponding revenues. The starting point or the initial investment requirement is not what really matters; it is the impact that additional (fixed) costs and complexity will have on the company's total cost structure if the business picks up. With that definition, scalability can of course also apply in industries that produce physical goods with a lot of (fixed) operating assets.

Nevertheless, extreme scalability predominantly applies to knowledge-based or information-based industries where the incremental costs attached to each additional sales unit are virtually zero. IT, e-commerce, social networks, electronic or online payment services – these are industries where you definitely find companies with perfectly scalable business models.

And although scalability is quite a structural phenomenon, heavily depending on the nature of the value proposition and the related business model, it can also be traced back to the management's organisation skills and the quality of the firm's operating processes. A firm's leadership can actively improve efficiency and mitigate complexity via a good process management. A reasonable and mindful input of assets and also a smart use of manpower help to keep the fixed cost-requirements in check and, even more important in this context here, to hold the total cost curve down even when the business really spurts upwards. By taming costs and complexity, some firms can literally suppress their total cost curve at every level of business activity.

Lastly, the value of (inorganic) growth from acquisitions tends to be not very high overall and ranks lowest in terms of profitability compared to the other growth types.

For the acquiring firm, it is often not the current ROIC of the target company that is the actual trigger for a merger but the long-term perspective to expand its negotiation power together as an amalgamated conglomerate after the deal. Access to new or complementary technology, bigger scale, or wider scope, just to name the most evident, are competitive advantages that can buttress the bargaining position of such transformed players in the capitalistic game.

Nonetheless, the buyer in an acquisition is obliged to make all the capital investments up front. In addition, these advance payments to the seller include the expected cash flows from the target plus a premium to stave off other bidders. So apart from the risk that the desired effects from the deal do not materialise (i.e., the invested money does not create any (sufficient) value in return), a lot of the value potential the buyer sees in the target company is already handed over to the selling party at the very beginning.

For that reason, although there is usually always a kind of best owner,[81] even such a firm has mostly a hard time subsequent to the buy to make the overall

---

[81] The **best owner** is the organisation or company that is able to get the highest shareholder value (i.e., net cash flow) out of a certain business on a sustainable basis. Sources for best ownership are, for instance, unique synergies between business lines as well as distinctive skills that the best owner can bring to a (new) business. Tim Koller, Richard Dobbs, and Bill Huyett, *Value: The Four Cornerstones of Corporate Finance* (Hoboken, New Jersey: John Wiley & Sons, 2011).

goal of the merger a reality and to earn an attractive return for itself in relation to the paid acquisition premium.[82]

Sustaining (Revenue) Growth

It's crucial to understand that sustaining a high growth rate of the revenues is much more difficult for a company than sustaining a high ROIC. The math is simple. Suppose the underlying core product market is growing at an overall rate of, e.g., 5 percent per annum, and your company has currently $ 10 billion in revenues. Ten years from now, assuming your firm grows further at the same pace as the market, its revenues will be circa $ 16.3 billion. However, if it aspires to outperform the average market and to grow organically even at 8 percent per annum, in ten years the revenues will need to be circa $ 21.6 billion, $ 5.3 billion more than if it was growing at 5 percent per annum. Not talking about the likely resistance from the competition, the issue is obvious here: even if the product markets are growing at "only" 5 percent per annum - where is your undertaking going to find that magnitude of growth?

Considering this major hurdle, many companies have unrealistic growth targets. As an investor, you should scrutinise these goals and do the math. Often, you will find that you would have paid too much for

---

[82] The so-called *winner's curse*. This effect suggests that the buying party regularly pays too much for what it gets in return. The reasons behind this seem to be incomplete information about the true (i.e., intrinsic) value of the acquisition target as well as a lack of self-control in the heat of the battle. Rolf Dobelli, *The Art of Thinking Clearly* (London: Sceptre, 2013).

The Valuation

growth. Sustaining growth over the long run is not only very hard but often impossible, due to the natural limitations of the markets' sizes.

In the end, the size and the growth of a company are constrained by the size of each of its product or service markets as well as the number of different product or service markets in which it contends. ExxonMobil, for instance, derived the chief part of its revenues in the last few years from two products in large markets – crude oil and natural gas. Procter & Gamble, representing the other extreme, reached its revenues in the same time by competing in hundreds of smaller product markets.

Another limitation to unlimited growth lies in the fact that almost all products and services have natural life cycles. Given this natural life cycle of products and services, the only true way for a company to achieve high growth is to continually find new products or services, geographic markets, or customer segments. A company needs to enter such untouched areas early enough to capture a potential competitive advantage within and to enjoy their most profitable (because less competitive) high-growth phase. The bigger the company gets, generally, the more difficulties it will have to keep the same growth rate of the revenues, due to the described absolute limitations.

Regardless of the constraints, the growth in the revenues still varies considerably across the companies in the same industry, as you also might have noticed at the stock markets. To sustain high growth, companies need to overcome the portfolio treadmill effect. For each product or service that has matured and declined in revenues, the company is under pressure to find a similar-sized replacement product or service to keep the same level of revenues – and even more in order to continue growing its top line. But finding sizable new sources of growth requires more experimentation and a longer time horizon through which many companies are not willing to invest. General Electric's GE Capital business was a side business in the early 1980s, when it generated about 8 percent of General Electric's total profits. After twenty-six years of consistent investment, it reached nearly half of General Electric's total profits.

Thus, even though the importance of growth in revenues is undeniable, large companies must have discipline and patience – discipline to select only the types of growth that will create the most value and patience to nurture new growth platforms over many years.[83]

Capital Costs

It's in the nature of things – a firm requires cash to start and run its operations. The respective funding mainly comes from the outside as equity and bank loans into a company but can be internally generated in the form of (interest-free) trade payables towards suppliers or via pension plans too.

For a company, capital costs are the costs to be paid to all its security holders (i.e., investors like shareholders and banks) on average in order to finance its assets and daily operations.

---

[83] Tim Koller, Richard Dobbs, and Bill Huyett, *Value: The Four Cornerstones of Corporate Finance* (Hoboken, New Jersey: John Wiley & Sons, 2011).

The Valuation

To understand the magnitude of a firm's capital costs in general and their impact on its value, it helps to understand the motivations of the primary capital providers, namely the shareholders and banks.

Capital costs fundamentally consist of two elements – one is about the **time value of money** for the individual capital provider. Whereas time as a physical parameter might be equal to every one of us, it has different implications to each individual if it comes to money and investing. As a basic principle, you can either invest (i.e., save) or consume your money. Consequently, when you invest, you need to postpone your consumption to the future. But consumption is, in the end, the reason why we all work and earn money.

Assuming that consuming something today is more important and joyful for a normal human being than consuming the same tomorrow, the deferring of consumption to the future has to have an outbalancing benefit in return.[84]

Moreover, individuals tend to experience rising salary levels over their working lives. That makes the money earned today less valuable in relation to the prospective, in tendency, enhanced income streams.

Both factors - the human preference of immediate consumption and the ascending salary levels of an individual over his or her professional life - drive the time value of money and effectively request a price for time that comes in the form of interests. In other words, the investors will embed the time value of money in their return expectations, making any

---

[84] George Loewenstein, *Exotic Preferences: Behavioural Economics and Human Motivation* (New York: Oxford University Press, 2007).

positive net cash flow today essentially worth more than one coming in tomorrow.[85]

In conclusion, the time value of money has, (indirectly) via the investors' return expectations, a material impact on a company's capital costs and, ultimately, value.

You might agree that normally an individual will know best about his or her consumption preference and its likely income development. Hence, the time value of money is a highly subjective cost for each lender of capital, not an objective one that can be derived via a stiff formula.

The other element of the capital costs is reflecting the overall perils attached to a business and its cash flows – the ***investment risk***. Investment risk has to be defined as a threat to the investor to lose money, just as investment return is defined as an opportunity for the investor to make money. Yes, companies have different sets of risk and return, from all the good reasons I have elaborated in this book so far, resulting in every instance in unique cash flow patterns. And both aspects of any business, risk and return, are simultaneously considered when we make investment decisions.

People generally tend to be risk averse; the higher the risk, the more return is required to make them invest. If a business exposes big threats, you would only engage yourself with an investment if it also promises high (i.e., risk adequate) returns in exchange - that is purely economic rationale. So the

---

[85] Carl Menger, *Principles of Economics* (USA: Skyler J. Collins, 2012).

capital costs of a company on principle embody the appetite for risk and return of its investors too.

Taking a slightly changed viewpoint, capital costs for a firm can also be labelled **opportunity costs** for the respective investors as they constantly compare the different offerings in the market and put their money where the relation between risk and return is most attractive to them. When comparing alternatives, see that an investment at least has to bring the same return as the next possible opportunity if the risks attached are identical. More risks will require more return as compensation, depending on the individual investor's attitude towards risk.

As one result, companies are in (indirect) competition for external funding resources with other investment opportunities. Having a low-risk, profitable business running means then to have a high degree of negotiation power towards the money lenders.

But the returns that the equity shareholders and banks ask for depend not only on the business model and its inherent risks and chances. As explained a little earlier as well, individual knowledge, subjective risk awareness, and the time horizon of each investor also determine what the capital costs for the company will finally be.

By offering securities, something that especially banks put emphasis on, and also by enhancing transparency to all its investors, a company's top management can actively decrease the capital costs. In addition, running operations in a safe way can lower capital costs at long sight; when operational risks are reduced, operational excellence pays off in this regard too.

Step Two: Estimating Value

Valuation and the whole stock investing story are not exact science. The discipline of valuation is more a set of heuristics, logic, business acumen, scepticism, life experience, and insights into economics such as competitive advantages. There are just too many parameters to consider, making it virtually impossible to derive an exact, universal value with one mechanical formula.

But this is not dramatic. Valuation is nevertheless a key activity in investing. The goal is just not to get a precise figure at the end but a reasonable price assessment from your standpoint, indicating if the market is pricing the stock too high or too low at some point in time. Once you have arrived at a reasonable figure, all you can do is wait till the market gives you the opportunity to buy at or even below that estimated fair price.

With that, valuation and stock investing are primarily not about over- or undervalued stocks. An investor first has to determine what he or she wants to earn and what risk he or she is willing to take, respectively. Next, the investor needs to assess the amounts and certainty of cash flows from the potential investment to him or her. The result is the fair price in the eyes of the individual investor; all that is left to do then is to wait stoically for that "right" price at the stock market.

The Valuation

So in the first place, you as an investor have to be reasonably correct about future profitability and related cash flows of a company.

But, yes, stock investing is also a game you play against the other participants at the bourse. It is about all estimations regarding future prospects – yours and the market's. The market's opinion about a firm's outlook is reflected in the current stock prices. Take this as your benchmark and challenge the assumptions behind. If you do have a correct view of the matter and conservative return expectations, a wonderful business can become a fruitful investment to you on days when there is a temporary sell-off at the stock markets.

To come to a reasonable estimation for the value of a stock, there are basically three major types of concepts for valuing companies out there: present-value concepts derived from discounted cash flows, price multiples / yields, and capital return-based approaches. In all these concepts, the same three major elements of value estimation mentioned before come into play: your personal return / risk expectation, the future cash flow pattern, and the traded stock price.

All three types of valuation concepts are useful and indispensable parts of the investing toolkit, and the wise investor will apply more than one to an eventual stock purchase.

Estimating Value via the *Net Present Value Concept*

In finance, the **net present value** (**NPV**) is defined as the sum of the present values of incoming and outgoing cash flows over a period of time. In other words, the net present value concept accounts for the time value of money - the fact that timing has an impact on the value of cash flows.

If it comes to stocks, calculating a present value can be a complex, hence, inexact process as it includes many vague assumptions concerning short- and long-term growth rates, capital expenditures, return requirements, and others. Naturally, it is impossible to predict all these variables with perfect precision.

But that should not stop us. Despite its challenges, the net present value concept can provide a good estimate of what we should spend today to have an investment worth a certain amount of money at a specific point in the future. Your knowledge and insight about the customer value, the related business model, and hopefully existing favourable economics such as competitive advantages will help you to make a reasonably accurate guess about a firm's future prospects.

The outcome of your estimation process will be an *intrinsic value* that represents, in your eyes, the *fair price* for a certain company. All an investor needs to do then is to compare his or her estimate with the market's estimate (i.e., the current stock market price for the company). And in case the market sells shares of that company well below the fair price, a clever investor buys on that day.

The Valuation

Cash Flows in the NPV Concept

The lifeblood of value and hence the basis of the NPV concept are cash flows.

Free cash flow to the firm (***FCFF***) is one of the most common cash flows used in NPV concepts.[86] In this case, the stock investor needs to deduct debt and add the cash position from the discounted cash flow amount at the date of the valuation. But as FCFF is a mix of cash flows, all owned by different capital providers, the individual stock investor's stake is not always that clear.

Therefore, ***free cash flow to equity*** (***FCFE***) might be the better choice from an equity investor's perspective as it represents the cash flow exclusively to the shareholders, not only after operational spending and investments but also after debt measures.[87] FCFE is most meaningful if the respective company is profitable and its borrowing is stable. And because it is the firm's cash flow exclusively to you as

---

[86] There are a number of different paths you can use in order to directly or indirectly calculate FCFF, but the most straightforward formula is as follows: EAT + interests * (1 − (cash operating) tax rate) + depreciation and amortization + other non-cash charges −/+ changes in working capital −/+ changes in net fixed asset investments. The term (EAT + interests * (1 − (cash operating) tax rate)) is the **net operating result after taxes** (***NOPAT***); it represents the EAT of a company if it would be financed at 100 percent with equity. Also: NOPAT = EBIT * (1 − (cash operating) tax rate).

[87] In essence, the difference between FCFF and FCFE is just the debt services and the changes of the position net borrowing. Hence, FCFE = EAT + depreciation and amortization + other non-cash charges −/+ changes in working capital −/+ changes in net fixed asset investments +/− changes in net borrowing.

a (potential) shareholder, it can be straightforwardly discounted with your personal discount factor.[88]

As mentioned earlier, a great danger in stock investing is paying too much for (revenue) growth. An interesting variant of FCFE to help you is **owner's earnings**, which tell you what cash flow will be obtainable for you as a shareholder in the equilibrium or mature state of the respective company. To get this figure, you start with the EAT of the latest period available[89] and add back depreciation, amortization, and other non-cash charges. That would be the same start as when calculating FCFE. If the company then requires additional working capital to maintain its competitive position and unit volume, this increment should be considered as well.

After this, the investor needs to estimate and reflect the fixed-asset investments in the equilibrium state of the company. In contrast to FCFE, which contemplates the total capital expenditures, owner's earnings just include the part for the maintenance. So the owner's earnings are FCFE after maintenance capital expenditures only. The rationale behind this is that merely the capital expenditures for maintenance works are required to keep the ongoing business competitive and running.

---

[88] In case the company sees a material growth phase in the next few years, it makes sense to include detailed periods in your model and to put the equilibrium state at the end in the period for the terminal value then. If the company is already in its steady state, you can directly apply the perpetuity formula on the average annual cash flows of this phase.

[89] The latest available period might be the latest actual or the most recent annual projection of the company's financials.

The Valuation

With all this, in order to estimate owner's earnings, an investor will not only have to have a good idea about the firm's spending musts in its mature phase but also has to practically split these total capital expenditures into the categories "growth" and "maintenance" and subtract the latter one in the cash flow calculation.

Furthermore, please keep in mind also that spending for maintenance can enhance ROIC via improvements in the field of operational excellence and with that can create additional value. Consequently, not only the capital expenditures required to keep up the unit volume or output levels but also the money spending necessary to sustain the firm's long-term competitive position have to be allocated to the category "maintenance". You can also put it the other way round – only the capital expenditures that create value via additional business and related revenues must be neglected in the calculation of owner's earnings. To arrive finally at owner's earnings, please cater at the end of the calculation for the borrowing needs (i.e., changes in debt levels) as you would do for FCFE.

By representing ultimately an estimation of cash flow to equity in the mature (i.e., equilibrium) phase of a company, owner's earnings can lead to a kind of benchmark price for you in order to avoid paying too much for (revenue) growth.

But although the concept is compelling, a few critical points demand your attention. To start with, in most legislations, companies are not required to report "growth" and "maintenance" capital expenditures separately. Being in a sense the midpoint of the owner's earnings concept, this aspect especially requires that the investor knows the content of a firm's capital budget very well. It might be possible for a company to make this distinction by itself, but an investor would rarely get this information and hence would face the challenge to find a workaround. If such separation is not available via a (credible) company presentation or another information source, a passable proxy for maintenance capital expenditures might be an average over the past few years' depreciation and amortization expenses; assuming the total asset base was somewhat stable and proportions are somehow known. Unfortunately, this simplifying approach leads to the next issue. By taking the past average of the total depreciation and amortization as an approximation for future maintenance spending, the investor assumes that the hitherto existing pattern will remain stable going forward; sometimes this is just not true.

Thus, an investor's good insight and logic are required in order to prevent inconsistencies. Inflation, changes in technology, and developments in the competitive field usually should be part of the estimation process for maintenance spending.

Yet despite these weak points, which can all be properly addressed by an intelligent investor, the owner's earnings represent a meaningful concept that can assist you in getting a rational idea about a company's net value in its steady state. By anchoring your fair price expectation to this figure, you will pretty likely not pay too much for the projected growth of a business.

Discount Factor in the NPV Concept

As much as there seems to be a common agreement about the concept of time value of money and the necessity to discount future cash flows for that, there are some quite different views about the other element of capital costs, namely investment risk.

In today's financial industry practise, investment risk gets calculated objectively via mathematical formulas and statistics. **Weighted average costs of capital (WACC)** and **capital asset pricing model (CAPM)** are widely spread concepts that try to derive the capital costs and related discount factor via statistics and mathematical formulas from past data.

But despite their popularity in the financial industry, which is mainly derived from their simplicity and utility, WACC and CAPM have one issue in common – they both are not working in reality. Agreed, investors deserve a rate of return that compensates them for taking on risk. But while trying to have an objective way to calculate capital costs and a respective discount factor, some people forgot logic. In order to have a technically working approach, they took two erroneous shortcuts. It is these two daring assumptions, on which WACC and CAPM are based, that make them useless for an intelligent investor – the assumption of market efficiency and the relevance of past information in order to predict the future.

Free of any doubt, WACC and CAPM have several flaws from a single investor's point of view.

First, WACC represents an average picture of all capital providers. But as successful investing is not a team sport, WACC can't be the discount factor for you as an individual investor.

Second, the WACC formula asks you to use market values as weights for the different capital components, be they actual ones or estimates of future ones. But the equity portion is what we are ultimately after – how can I have this information ex ante as a weight, at this point of the valuation process? This issue represents a classic circular reference problem, a Gordian knot that can't be cut with the measures we currently have at hand.

Third, to derive weights from current market values (i.e., stock prices) is misleading. At long sight, the market might get it right, hence bringing price and value in sync. In the short term and often also in the mid run, however, the markets produce inefficient results (i.e., stock prices). With all this, taking a current stock price as a proxy for the weight of the equity costs in WACC can be completely distorting.

Fourth, in many (standard) models, the discount factor WACC decreases when debt levels rise. Many investors live under the impression that, just by financing projects with more debt, they can actively decrease the respective investment hurdle rates. In this logic, a decreasing WACC in the course of more bank loans would mean less risk for all investors in total. But this thinking is way too short-sighted. No matter what the financial leverage, the total risk of a business can't change. No other party is taking risk from the shoulders of the capital providers only because more debt is used to run the shop. Hence, WACC, the average return requirement of all investors in total, generally can't change only when debt levels vary.[90]

Fifth, the WACC formula contains the **beta factor** as measure for equity investment risk. I have no idea what the theoretical reasons and good intentions might have been to introduce this concept to the investment world – it makes really no sense in investment practice. Beta is simply a statistic measure for volatility in stock prices,[91] derived from past data. In the model, higher volatility translates then into higher equity investment risks and, subsequently, higher WACC. But risk definitely doesn't equate the volatility of stock prices from an investor's angle, and (future) risk can't be estimated by using past information. Volatility might be a helpful indicator for the extremity of emotions or swings in the mood of the stock exchange. But once again, the major risk for an investor is to lose money – no matter if the stock prices of the respective investments swing more or less over time. So you are not facing investment risk unless you sell when stocks are down after a panic attack in the herd. In addition, risks attached to a business change over time, and challenges ahead will always differ from the challenges already behind. You will never be able to tell the future by simply extrapolating history. Thus,

---

[90] More sophisticated valuation models incorporate this aspect via a variation in the beta factor; in effect, then, WACC is not affected by changing debt levels within a certain range.

[91] Compared to an appropriate benchmark (i.e., the **market portfolio**). In practice, professional investors often chose an equity market index like the S&P 500 as a proxy. In theory, however, the market portfolio should contain all investable assets. But this in turn would lead to further issues like the fact that for many assets like real estate, stamp collections, or precious metals, prices and returns are hard to obtain or unobservable.

the investor's risk can't be priced by plainly adding a percentage for (past) volatility on the discount factor; that just does not work, irrespective of how sophisticated the underlying approach might appear to you. The past is a pretty good indicator for the future if it comes to human behaviour, but stock prices are not made by that in the long term. Hence, relying on the past performance of stocks in order to predict their future is not working.

With all this, at least one thing might be clear to you now – CAPM and WACC do not help us to calculate investment risk, capital costs, and a related discount factor. The WACC and CAPM concepts are only compelling in theory. But what works in theory does not necessarily work in practise. It is the flawed logic as well as the calculation method of most components of WACC and CAPM that unfortunately make them, in essence, useless for investment purposes.

You might counter that the whole investing community works with this concept – a sad fact that should not make you join this foolish herd. Running with the crowd is most often an inappropriate behaviour pattern – and so it is here. You might further argue and consider WACC and CAPM as the only concepts available and that it might be better to apply this than nothing.[92] I would respectfully object and claim the polar opposite: in this case, it might be

---

[92] A classic example for the ***availability bias*** in the stock investing process: people prefer wrong information to no information (i.e., a wrong "map" to no "map") just in order to have the "good" feeling that decisions have been based on something "reliable". Rolf Dobelli, *The Art of Thinking Clearly* (London: Sceptre, 2013).

The Valuation

better to have no approach at hand at all rather than one based on these misleading concepts.

Individual capital costs and related investment risk can't be calculated with a generic, objective concept. And even if it would be possible, in my opinion that risk should not be put into the discount factor of a company's cash flows.

To be quite frank with you, an investor should not try to anticipate investment risk via the discount factor at all. Seriously; it just does not do the trick. And it might not make sense either. Even if you discount very risky or improbable figures with an astronomically high discount factor, your investment risk does not vanish. Yes, you might buy lower then as the net present value gets discounted more and reduce investment risk that way. But you lose the feeling for the fair price of the stock. Your discount factor should not include a premium for investment risk because there is no way to quantify it prior to the real event.

Consequently, in case there are some significant risks in the figures that necessitate consideration, I suggest working with a scenario analysis. By estimating the best, the base, and the worst case of a business, you will get a more reliable idea about the most probable state of a company in the future. Doing so, you can reasonably estimate the impact of certain events on value in case they would occur.

In principle, there are only two ways to mitigate investment risk at this stage of the stock investment process: via a solid understanding of the business and a lower purchase price for the shares.

Therefore, the discount factor, from an intelligent

investor's standpoint, should merely reflect the individual opportunity costs in terms of time, or better, a compensation for the delay of consumption. As the investment approach described in this book needs time, you should take long-term bond rates available in the market that mature decades from now. The longer the term to maturity of the respective bonds, the better, as our general intention is to hold the stocks forever. With that, an investor should opt for a risk-free, long-term rate like the thirty-year US Treasury bond yield or the thirty-year German government bond yield; both can do the job in principle, depending just on what your individual currency environment is. The current yield of default risk-free thirty-year US Treasury bond yield, for instance, reflects the time horizon of a long-term stock investor and represents for him or her the best and risk-free alternative to a stock investment.[93]

And in case you might seek a further reduction of your investment risk, a lump-sum discount on the finally calculated net present value is a rational approach. As this again is a very personal decision that directly and only relates to your subjective attitude towards (investment) risk, you will have to define the magnitude of this discount factor by yourself.

In my experience, such **margin of safety** can range from -20 percent to -50 percent on the calculated NPV in the base case, depending on the individual's risk aversion.

---

[93] If it comes to a foreign investment, an investor might consider additional macro-economic factors in the discount factor, mainly inflation or interest rate differentials.

The Valuation

All in all, that way the whole (theoretical) discussion about "appropriate" discount factors is brought back to practical levels, leaving more time to look at what really matters – the operational business with its current economics and future prospects.[94]

Estimating Value via Earnings and Cash Flow-Based Multiples and Yields

Two other tools in your valuation kit box should be multiples and yields.

To start with, **multiples** are simply an expression of a market value (i.e., a stock price) relative to a key statistic that is assumed to relate to that value. To be meaningful, that statistic, whether earnings or cash flows, must bear a logical relationship to the stock price observed. In other words, it needs to be a relevant factor for that stock price. Earnings can be

---

[94] To arrive at a fair stock price of a company in its steady state as per today, I just apply the perpetuity formula, with the average annual FCFE in the nominator and a current thirty-year government bond yield in the denominator. The result (i.e., the present (equity) value of the company) then gets divided by the average number of fully diluted, outstanding shares. Unlike basic outstanding shares, fully diluted shares include all possible sources of conversion to outstanding shares, such as convertible bonds, stock options, stock warrants, and convertible preferred stock or debt, assuming these securities were exercised. Finally, I always deduct a lump-sum -25 percent margin of safety in order to reduce my overall investment risk. In case of visible growth, I use a two-stage approach. In the growth period, I model the accretive business in a detailed manner. Then, I also try to (conservatively) estimate the FCFE of the company in its future, mature state and apply the perpetuity formula on that terminal value. All the resulting cash flows get also discounted by a risk-free interest rate and trimmed by my margin of safety in a last step.

used as a statistic, assuming a strong, positive correlation between earnings and resulting cash flows. But because accounting can distort that correlation quite a bit over some time, any investor is well advised to check if the earnings really express cash flows in an adequate manner before using them for valuation purposes.

Multiples are often criticised as being too simplistic, as they combine many value drivers into one single-point estimate. With that, it gets difficult for an investor to disaggregate the effects of the various value drivers of a business. That might be true if you start your valuation directly with a multiple and try then to drill down from there to a firm's value drivers. But as you have already built a solid understanding about the business (i.e., potential investment) earlier, by decomposing ROE and ROIC, multiples can be a worthwhile measure for you at this point of the valuation process.

You should use earnings or cash flows on average levels or even better, in equilibrium, as such statistics veritably indicate the long-term value potential of a company. By putting annual earnings or cash flows to shareholders per share in relation to the current stock price, an investor will basically get a relative price indication for the stock, expressed in years. Having this dimension, multiples (i.e., relative prices) can be compared between direct rivals, across time, or industries.

Another advantage of multiples is their practicality. Not only is the current stock price accessible at any time, but also there are various options easily available for the statistic in the denominator.

EBITDA, for example, can be used in a multiple as a very rough proxy for FCFF under strict preconditions. Most important, investments in working capital and fixed assets should not be material or at least stable over time. Furthermore, EBITDA only works from the equity investor's perspective if net debt is insignificant relative to the company's total value and if the financial leverage is expected to be constant in the future due to a strong and reliable business model. Otherwise, a change in capital structure might falsify the multiple. Lastly, please see that EBITDA does not reflect the cash taxes paid by the firm.

Therefore, in the optimum and in order to sidestep flaws due to accounting, an investor should directly try to estimate the FCFF or FCFE and put that figure on a per-share basis into relation to the current stock market price. Apart from this and as discussed earlier, the owner's earnings represent the FCFE of a firm in its mature state. Using owner's earnings in a multiple will give you a conservative, relative value for the stock investment you are taking into consideration.

There is definitely some merit to a multiple-based valuation, as long as you do not go about it blindly and always keep in mind what a wonderful business basically is: an easy (i.e., low-risk) value proposition within a good (i.e., well-designed) business model around a strong and hence stable or even rising customer demand, safeguarded by powerful and durable competitive advantages.

An undertaking trading at a lower multiple than others in the same industry might be a good opportunity – or it might deserve that lower financial ratio as it has a lower quality in the revenues, a less attractive business model, dubious growth prospects, or weak / non-existent competitive advantages.[95] With that, a multiple might not directly show you the reason for a stock trading low or high, but it can give you a hint to intensify your analysis of the respective company and its value drivers.

If multiples are turned from head to toe (i.e., earnings or cash flows are divided by a stock's price), we get another handy valuation measure – **yields**. Being the exact reciprocal of a multiple, a yield gives you the (annual) return from your investment in percentages.

For instance, using net earnings and the current market value of equity (i.e., the stock price) in a yield measure gives you a kind of "market ROE" - the estimated return on your equity investment if you buy at that price level. Such yield can be compared to a risk-free investment alternative such as long-term US Treasuries. The delta between the risk-free rate and the current stock yield would be your (additional) return requirement in order to accept the equity

---

[95] It's worthwhile to mention that (excessive) financial leverage also can lower a multiple. The higher (bankruptcy) risk, stemming from more fixed costs (i.e., fixed interests and instalments) for the firm, finds its expression in a lower stock valuation (i.e., lower multiple) by the market. Once more, it becomes evident that financial leverage does not drive value but only steps results as well as risks up. Tim Koller, Richard Dobbs, and Bill Huyett, *Value: The Four Cornerstones of Corporate Finance* (Hoboken, New Jersey: John Wiley & Sons, 2011).

The Valuation

investment risk – a call you have to make on your own.

Finally, yields can illustrate in mathematical terms what successful stock investing is mainly about at this point of the process - knowing the business and buying low.

All you need is a reasonably accurate estimation about the true future cash flows of the firm to you as a shareholder as well as a clear-cut idea about your personal, subjective appetite for return and risk.

Earnings or cash flows divided by current stock price gives you the current yield of that stock. Setting your personal yield expectation into this equation and solving for stock price gives you the price you need to watch out for in order to realise your envisaged yield. All you can and have to do then is to wait for the stock market to offer you the respective opportunity to buy.

See again that knowing the business and its likely cash flow streams will help you to achieve your personal investment goals regarding risk and return. By buying low, you actively enhance the investment return potential and reduce the investment risk at the same time.

Also, you can add a margin of safety on top of your return requirements in order to cater for your subjective attitude towards risk. By adjusting your personal return requirement upwards, you are indirectly watching for even lower stock prices and, via that, reducing the investment risk further.

Estimating Value via Capital-Based Multiple Price-to-Book and ROE

The *price-to-book ratio* (*P/B ratio*) is another relative price measure that can be used to challenge the current market prices and to estimate shareholder value. A P/B ratio of two, for instance, means that you have to pay a premium of 100 percent for one unit of book equity, or two times the current book equity. You pay such an elevated price due to the hopefully healthy economics and auspicious prospects of the respective company.

Nevertheless, knowing how long it will take to "earn back" that premium under the prevailing conditions can provide you with a sound feeling if the absolute stock price is great, reasonably fair, or way too high for what you get in return.

For the calculation of the time span (i.e., relative price measure), the (current or average) capital return ratio ROE comes into play. Although it is ROIC at which a company prospers in total, ROE shows at which rate the shareholders' equity grows per annum. And although influenced by financing and accounting, ROE also expresses the profitability of the business, about which you should have a reasonably accurate opinion at this point.[96]

---

[96] Alternatively to the EAT you can use the (current or average) FCFE or owner's earnings in the nominator of ROE; that way, accounting does not influence the capital return ratio.

The Valuation

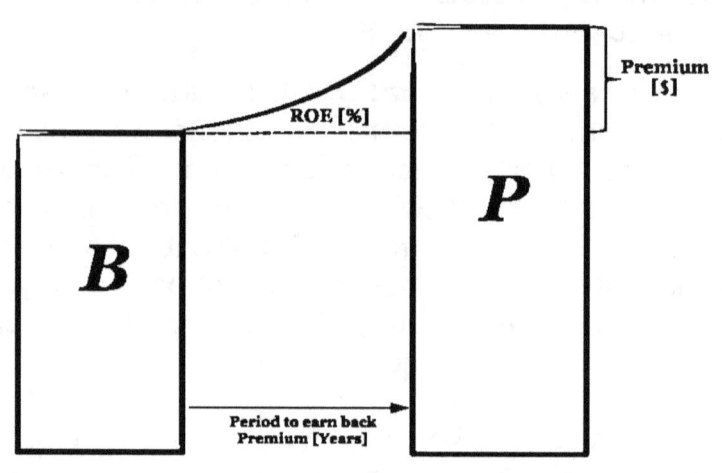

Exhibit 5.4 The Earn Back Period – P/B – Ratio and ROE

The approach assumes that the capital structure and financing ratios are kept stable by the company;[97] furthermore, the capital return rates as well as all relating value drivers[98] stay constant within the relevant period of time.

Then, the approach gives you how many years it takes a company with a certain profitability to build

---

[97] This means that the company pays no dividends and conducts no share buyback programs; all potential cash flows to the shareholders are used to run and grow the business. Agreed, especially for mature firms, these assumptions are tough. Nevertheless, if a steady-state company pays excess money out, this capital can, after all due taxes, be reinvested in additional stocks of the same company. That way, your total investment grows approximately at the prevailing ROE too.

[98] Mainly the high-quality and overall low-risk profile of the firm's value proposition and the corresponding business model, the strength of the underlying customer demand, its growth prospects, and, last but not least, the potent competitive position of the respective firm in the capitalistic game.

up shareholder value and to earn the paid equity investment premium back.[99]

No, the herewith described valuation logic does not deliver you an exact, fair price in absolute terms you can hunt for. But by translating one relative price (i.e., P times B) into another one (i.e., a time period like years), this method is worthwhile to you via other ways.

First, time is a physical dimension you might mentally get a better grip on rather than a financial ratio like P/B which, prima facie, does not mean anything from a valuation perspective. At least to me, a time period of eight years "to get my initial equity investment premium back" is more comprehensible than a plain P/B ratio of 5.1, for instance.

Second, by bringing capital return ratios another time into the picture, we can make use of our previous analysis of profitability and value. All the work done there can be used here as well in order to challenge the stock price from another angle. The underlying subject-matter is therefore again nothing else but analysing and understanding a business, its profitability, and the corresponding value development.

Third, the approach illustrates the power of the compound interest effect and implies with this once

---

[99] If you want to estimate how many years it will take you to double your invested money at a certain rate of return, including the compounding interest effect, you can use the ***rule of seventy-two***. Let's say you can invest your money at a return rate of 8 percent. Now simply divide seventy-two by eight; the result is nine. In other words, it will take you nine years to double your investment at a return rate of 8 percent if all yields are reinvested during that time.

more the basic necessity to be invested in reliably profitable businesses over numerous years in order to have investment success in a sustainable manner.

Like earnings or cash flow-based multiples, the "equity investment premium earning back period" is also comparable between peers, across industries, or over time. That way, the concept will substantiate your opinion about the reasonable or fair stock price to be paid for a certain firm and its business.

Sit and Wait

My general intention with this whole chapter was to give you some ideas about value analysis and estimation. I basically listed everything I look for in order to understand a firm's value and to come at the end of the estimation process to a reasonable (i.e., fair) price for it.

It is OK to stop at this stage. If the "right" or fair price does not show up, you need to sit and wait for your "right" moment. That is how it works with stock investing – patience is a key discipline you need to master.[100]

---

[100] Throughout the whole stock investment process, people tend to fall victim to the **action bias**; they compensate eagerness, restlessness, and their inability to quickly judge a certain event or situation with headless hyperactivity. Please do not do this; do not rush decisions just in order to appear to be quick-witted or competent. Never lose your cool, always think at first all the determining information through, and make your move only when you have understood a certain matter in extenso. Rolf Dobelli, *The Art of Thinking Clearly* (London: Sceptre, 2013).

But it can also be seen as a freedom of choice. In all fairness, opting not to buy can be a pretty satisfying decision too.

So you should not take every swing. Enjoy the valuation exercise to the full and, in principle, expect that you will only have a few really good investment opportunities in your whole life. You do not know when, but they will for sure turn up at some point in time. Therefore, all you can do is to be prepared, sit, and wait.

No doubt, the fear of missing an investment opportunity can be quite a psychological challenge. And regret when exactly that happens is truly such an unpleasant, irksome feeling.

Thus, sitting and waiting is definitely not easy and, of course, is much easier said than done. What can help you to rein in your impatience is a kind of "seed investment". By buying merely a small portion of the looked-for stock for the start, your (natural) hunting instinct and desire to possess might get tamed somewhat. Although the position is immaterial in absolute money terms, that small portion might already give you some intellectual satisfaction and psychological relaxation. You can be happy about your investment decision, at least a little bit, when the stock price rises; the alternative would be a big regret not possessing that stock at all. And if the stock price turns south, your loss is minor in absolute money terms.

In addition, you have the chance to significantly reduce your average purchase price for that stock position by buying more at lower price levels.

The Valuation

The temporary lower quotes and the transaction costs for the seed investment would be the price for suppressing your impatience and controlling your emotions. But all in all, you might find it easier with this little trick to bridge the time until the "right" purchasing price (i.e., the chance to buy in bulk) leaps into your view.

VI. The Holding Period

Sell Never or at least for the Right Reasons

At this stage of my investment approach, the active work becomes less, and it is time for you to take a seat in order to enjoy the trip. While monitoring your investments doing operationally pretty fine, please ignore the erratic ups and downs at the stock exchange that will naturally occur from time to time. The market is just doing its job, trying to find a fair level for the stock prices in a very emotional way.

Instead, focus on the horizon and stay convinced about your actions taken. The market will get it right in the long run; hence, the daily white noise at the stock exchange should really not bother you.

Also in the holding period, inactivity can be something very wise if done for the right reasons. By holding stocks over extended time spans, you will get over the mentioned noise and the accompanied short-term, downwards perils; your investment risk just diminishes along the way.

Apart from this, governments and banks constantly try to get their share of the pie. By holding investments with unrealised gains for a long time, you can forestall related taxes and save on transaction costs. Due to the time-value-of-money concept again, it generally makes big sense to postpone such payments to the future as much as possible.

In addition to the eased burden from taxes and

fees on your portfolio performance, you will unleash the real power engine for your stock investments to its full extent – the compound interest effect. By working day and night for you, putting returns on your returns, and so forth, the compound interest effect enables you to amass a surprisingly large net worth, even with only small investments constantly made over time. The results seem to be mingy in the beginning, but they keep coming in and snowball; the bulk of the compounded interest is actually piled up in the last third of the total holding period. With that, over the years, even minimal but steady investments can accumulate into a substantial wealth build-up. The only thing the compound interest effect asks from you is some patience so that it can really perform and show its awe-inspiring magic.

Albert Einstein is purported to have once remarked that the most powerful phenomenon in the universe is the compound interest; in addition, there are other nice stories around to illustrate the incredible potential of the compound interest effect.

One goes like this: very long ago, an Indian maharajah was so excited about the game of chess that he offered the inventor one wish. The inventor replied that he wanted one grain of rice on the first square of the chess board, two grains on the second, four on the third, and so on through to the sixty-fourth square. The unwitting maharajah immediately agreed to the prima facie, modest request. But two to the sixty-fourth power is over eighteen trillion grains of rice – more than enough to cover the entire surface of the earth.

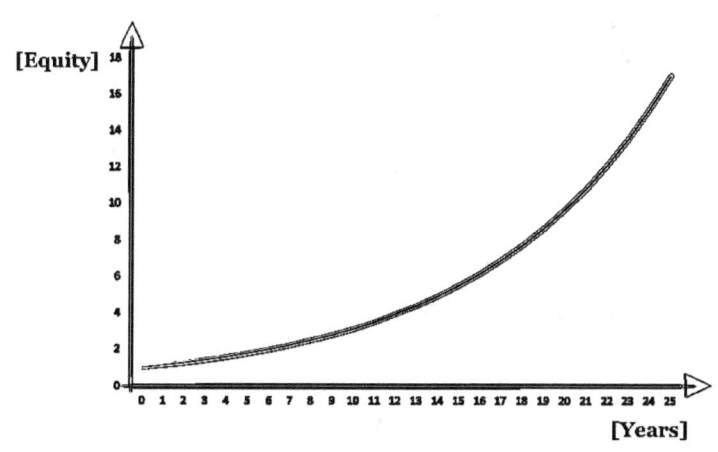

Exhibit 6.1 **The Compounding Interest Effect**

You can actually draw two key inferences from the graph above. First, even a small percentage accretion in the growth rate significantly boosts the returns over time. Second, the returns in the later years are more impressive due to the higher base effect. As compound growth is exponential, it substantially outperforms simple growth over longer periods of time.

The longer your holding period is, therefore, the more attractive your gains will be at the very end (i.e., over the total holding period).

I hope you agree that the compound interest effect can also do real wonders to your portfolio - if you just stick to your wonderful stocks long enough.

Thus, there is in reality only a short list of logical (i.e., perspicuous) reasons to sell the stock of a wonderful business at all:

1. Correction of a mistake
2. Fundamental changes within the game
3. Stock trades far above its intrinsic value
4. Better investment opportunities
5. Stock portfolio structure
6. Personal reasons

1. Correction of a Mistake

Finding out that your initial analysis and assumptions were incorrect is perhaps the most painful reason to sell. But if you missed something significant when you scrutinised a company at the outset, whatever it was, your original investment thesis very likely will not hold in reality. Maybe you thought the company had a very powerful and structural economic moat, but the competition nevertheless efficaciously managed to enter the business. Perhaps you analysed the business drivers of a company carefully and were reasonably sure that all would be working favourably for your potential investment before you bought, but you missed the one factor that counts the most and contradicts the whole investment idea.

No matter what the mistake was, it is rarely worthwhile hanging on to a stock that you bought based on a rationale that turns out to be erroneous or is no longer persuasive in the light of new, additional information. You should cut losses and move on in these cases.

It's fair to note here that a sell due to a mistake, especially in a loss situation, is far easier said than done. Most individuals tend to anchor their emotions to the price at which the stock was bought, and everybody hates losing money. [101] Actually, numerous psychological studies have proven that people generally experience almost twice as much (mental) pain when they lose money than joy they experience when the exact same amount is gained.

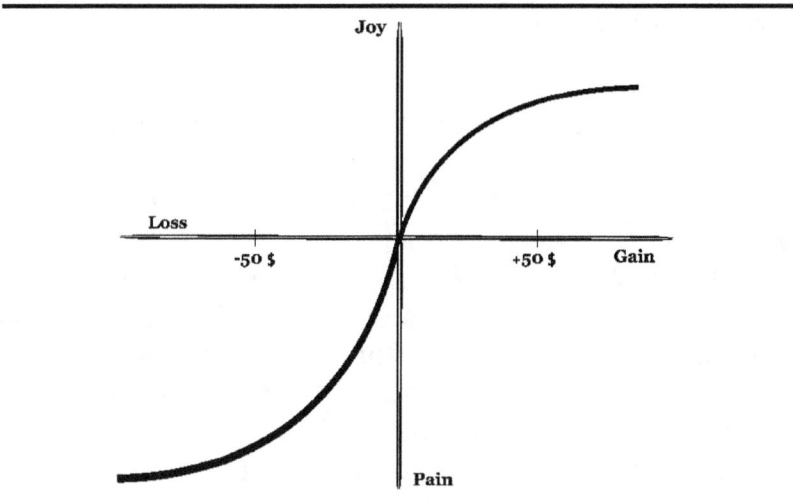

Exhibit 6.2 **Asymmetric Utility Function**

---

[101] Relates also to the **sunk cost fallacy**. The more we have already invested in something, be it time, effort, or money, the greater our urge to continue becomes. This irrational behaviour is driven by a natural need for consistency; consistency signifies credibility. A change in behaviour (e.g., admitting a mistake or selling a non-performing share), in contrast, makes us feel bad; we find contradictions to our previous actions and thoughts abominable. Daniel Kahneman, *Thinking, Fast and Slow* (London: Penguin Books, 2012). Terry Burnham and Jay Phelan, *Mean Genes* (New York: Penguin Books, 2001).

Due to that natural behaviour pattern, people just focus on the buying price for a stock, which is irrelevant information and has nothing to do with the future prospects of the respective firm. The investment return at that point in time solely depends on the corresponding economic outlook of the company, not on the initial stock price. So instead of challenging bygone events, the investor should give all attention to the more relevant information, such as the fact that the original assessment of the company's future may have been flat-out wrong.

A good trick to circumvent anchoring and loss aversion is this: each time you contemplate buying a stock, write down why you want to possess it and what you expect to happen with the company's operational and financial results. Such an **investment rationale statement** is not about quarterly earnings forecasts but the big picture of all relevant success factors for the company and its business. Why are you convinced about the company's value proposition? Is the respective business model sound? Do you see the sales growth at least to be steady or even to accelerate? Do you expect profit or capital return margins to go up for some solid reason? Do you see durable and wide-stretched economic moats that make the company a winner in the long run? Does the company dominate its value chain for some lasting reasons? All these assumptions should be written down by you - before the actual stock purchase.

Then, if the company nevertheless takes a negative turn, pull out your piece of paper and study whether your justification for being long in that particular stock is still a good idea. If it is, hold on or buy even more. But if it is not, selling is your only rational option – regardless of whether the stock quotations are up or down since the initial purchase. Your document will help you to stay objective rather than getting too emotional in a negative way when making your decision.

Face your faults, be honest with yourself, take action, and change to the better. It just does not make sense to hope that a stock will develop properly despite the fact that your working assumptions are not cogent. This would become wishful thinking and would only be about pure luck then; not really a profound basis for a professional investment style. At the same time you keep your money at risk while holding the wrong stock, it could do better in another investment where your analysis is right.

Done in a disciplined way, the right selling helps you to mitigate investment risks and to enhance investment returns for your overall stock portfolio at the same time.

2. Fundamental Changes within the Game

After several years of agglomerating net worth, the rocketing company you once bought has started to slow down in performance. Cash is piling up as the company has a tough time finding new, profitable areas to grow. Even worse, its negotiation power is fading away somehow as competition is creeping in from all angles, gnawing at the firm's nice capital return margins.

The Holding Period

Signs like these should give you the starting shot to reassess the company's fundamental economics and future prospects. If the current state and outlook are substantially worse than they used to be, it is time to sell.

The earlier-mentioned investment rationale statement would give you a good support again, this time not by comparing your original reasons with facts that have already materialised but with what is going to happen. Fortunately, the decision to sell after several years of success with a certain stock is not as painful as it would be in a loss situation. Nevertheless, once you are in a stock, return and risk of a stock investment can only be managed by constantly assessing the company's future projections and making a judgment based on that. If the potential for negative effects on value from future risks overpowers the chances for a further swelling of the firm's net worth, the only decision a good investor can make in order to safeguard the investment return and mitigate the investment risk is to divest the respective stock.

The alpha and omega of investing during the holding period is to constantly monitor the companies you own rather than the stock you own. The most excellent assessments are made from thinking like an entrepreneur.

Hence, it is far better to regularly spend some time gathering and interpreting the latest news about your companies rather than to look at the stock quotations twenty times a day.

3. Stock Trades Far above Its Intrinsic Value

Markets are made by facts and feelings. While in the long run the facts prevail, over the shorter periods of time it is often human behaviour and the related emotions that rule the stock exchange. Therefore, irrational, sometimes extreme swings in the stock prices happen naturally from time to time, to the downside as well as to the upside.

And so there are days the market might wake up in a splendid mood, offering you to pay a price far in excess of what your stock investment is really worth.

Frankly, there is nothing against taking advantage of other investors' good nature. Ask yourself how much more the market is willing to pay you compared to your estimate of the stocks' true value and how likely it is that your fair price gets topped even further by the market in the future.

Explicitly, I do not recommend right here to sell your stocks of wonderful companies just because they get a little pricey; the divesture would trigger taxes on capital gains as well as trading fees. And apart from these inevitable costs, you would no longer be taking advantage of the compound interest effect.

But the crucial point is that even the most wonderful businesses should be sold on days when their shares trade at egregious prices that do not reflect realistic values anymore.

4. Better Stock Investment Opportunities

Limited by the financial budget you can actually invest, you always want to be sure that your current stock investments yield the highest possible returns and reflect the greatest investment opportunities available at the bourse. So selling a modestly undervalued stock to fund the purchase of a "once-in-a-lifetime chance" is perfectly logical and economically worthwhile from an investor's point of view.

Of course, taxes and fees will come into play then, but if the emerging opportunity is significantly better than what you have at hand, it is absolutely OK to do the somewhat costly switch.

Anyway, as favourable investment occasions tend to be something of a rarity, you might not jump from stock to stock every week or month. If you find and trade more than one or two wonderful stocks a year, you must be already a damn good investor, or you should really look twice into the matter next time before changing horses.

5. Stock Portfolio Structure

Exceptional success with particular stocks can also trigger the need to restructure your stock portfolio. If one of your stocks performed strongly and much stronger than the rest of your portfolio, it may make sense to dial down the exposure a little bit and shrink the position in that stock. This is a very personal decision because some people actually favour more concentrated portfolios. The majority of stock investors, however, are more comfortable levelling the weights of the single positions in their portfolios to some extent. It simply does not make sense for some people having too many of their eggs in one basket. The diversification effect (i.e., the limitation of the investment risk from a portfolio perspective) is already properly achieved with eight single, equally-weighted stock positions. From twenty-five different stocks onwards, however, you will likely lose track of all the decisive matters. Hence, an optimally diversified stock portfolio should list not less than eight and not more than twenty-five company names.

In the end, it is your call. You have to be happy with your stock portfolio, and if keeping certain proportions makes you sleep better, so be it.

You should also take into consideration that your financial wealth does not only consist of stocks. Bonds, for example, are a proper asset class to grow your private net worth too. As bonds have a different risk / return profile than stocks, they might also develop differently in value over time, triggering once more the need to reallocate your money from time to time in your overall asset portfolio.

Also an alternative asset class like gold can be taken into account from a diversification standpoint. Gold does not actively create value, or put slightly different, produce cash, but it can help to stabilize the value of your overall portfolio in times when stock quotations fluctuate in an extreme way.

But again – this is all about your individual preferences.

6. Personal Reasons

Not only can companies, stocks, and portfolios change over time, but so can the investors themselves. The investment return you are asking for as an individual, as well as the risk you are willing and able to take for that, depend both largely on your personal circumstances and character traits.

Age, family status, or job – all of them matter when making decisions about investments as well as consumption in life.

Your age might not radically change your character traits but might make you a little wiser. With increasing age, people tend to take a more cautious or relaxed approach in general. They have seen and achieved meaningful things in life and want to preserve that status quo rather than to risk it in order to achieve even more.

Furthermore, you need your savings when you go into retirement. Temporary swings in stock prices in that kind of situation elevate the risk that you would not be able to sell without losses in some cases. Under such circumstances, (short-term) volatility can indeed represent an investment risk as you are somehow forced to monetise your stock positions. The length of the holding period actively mitigates investments risks in stocks. But when you are old, you do not have the time anymore to reduce this risk by just waiting for the efficiency of the markets and the compound interest effect to kick in.

Also, your family status has an influence on your life and decision-making style. Founding a family, for instance, is something wonderful too, but your financial degrees of freedom to have money invested in stocks get limited to some extent.

Moreover, you would like to be financially as flexible as possible once you have the responsibility for a family. Both aspects together will make you more cautious and less active at the bourse.

Another personal factor of relevance is your job – from a quantity as well as from a quality angle. How much you earn has, of course, a direct influence on your savings rate. Only if there is something left after the cost of living are you actually in the position to conduct investments and accumulate wealth. But also the kind of job you have picked enlarges or limits your possibilities to invest.

If you have a safe job within the public authorities (e.g., as a university professor), you might be able to aim for higher returns in investing. Instead of holding everything in cash and bonds, such individuals can definitely put more weight on stocks in their personal asset portfolio.

The opposite, however, is true if someone works in the industry as a manager, where large portions of his or her salary depend on the well-being of the company and, with that, also on the overall macro-economic picture. Exposed to a quite variable or better, unsure income stream, such a person should not seek additional volatility in his or her overall asset portfolio via stock investments. A more stable portfolio, consisting of cash and quality bonds, would be the better asset mix in such a setting.

Put Time on Your Side - and Grow with Your Stock Portfolio

Please keep in mind that holding stocks for many years is one fundamental pillar of my investment approach. By holding stocks over an extensive period of time, you get over the short-term downwards risks from the stock market's irrational behaviour, avoid unnecessary costs, and structurally benefit from the universal compound interest effect. That all not only boosts up your investment return at the end but also simultaneously decreases your investment risk very significantly over time.

True, holding a stock over the long haul is definitely easier said than done, as it requires discipline, focus on long-term goals, and insight into the compound interest effect. But as it just makes perfect sense, I hope you agree with me about the absolute necessity to keep stocks for long periods of time and to actually sell a wonderful business only under certain, exceptional circumstances.

The longer the holding period the better; so, I advise you to start with stock investments as soon as possible in your life. The earlier you begin, the more your returns will multiply, and the lower your risk to lose money is going to be.

Building up a prosperous stock portfolio takes considerable time, and as your overall investment budget might also be limited to some extent, other assets classes should be considered only after you have assembled a healthy flock of well-priced, wonderful businesses.

It might help you to think again like an entrepreneur. Success in business does not come overnight either. Why, then, should successful stock investing work that way? In order to be sustainably triumphant, you need to understand stock investing and doing business as a marathon, not as a sprint. Hence, please, do first things first and rejoice in this never-stopping journey.

Successful stock investing as described in this book is a life-long process, an endless lesson as well as an incessant intellectual exercise. And I hope it will enrich your life as it is doing mine.

"My favourite things in life don't cost any money. It's really clear that the most precious resource we all have is time."

(**Steve Jobs**)

Bibliography

Ackert, Lucy F. and Deaves, Richard, *Behavioral Finance: Psychology, Decision-Making and Markets* (Mason, Ohio: South-Western Cengage Learning, 2015).

Brilliant, Heather and Collins, Elizabeth, *Why Moats Matter: The Morningstar Approach to Stock Investing* (Hoboken, New Jersey: John Wiley & Sons, 2014).

Browne, Christopher H., *The Little Book of Value Investing* (Hoboken, New Jersey: John Wiley & Sons, 2007).

Burnham, Terry and Phelan, Jay, *Mean Genes* (New York: Penguin Books, 2001).

Calandro, Joseph Jr., *Applied Value Investing: The Practical Applications of Benjamin Graham's and Warren Buffet's Valuation Principles to Acquisitions, Catastrophe Pricing, and Business Execution* (USA: McGraw-Hill, 2009).

Campbell, Robin Alexander, *Seneca: Letters from a Stoic. Epistulae Morales ad Lucilium* (London: Penguin Books, 1969).

Christensen, Clayton M., *The Innovator's Dilemma: The Revolutionary Book that Will Change the Way You Do Business* (New York: HarperBusiness Essentials, 2003).

Clason, George S., *The Richest Man in Babylon* (New York: Signet, 1988).

Coleman, Thomas S., *A Practical Guide to Risk Management* (USA: Research Foundation of CFA Institute, 2011).

Copeland, Thomas E., Weston, J. Fred, and Shastri, Kuldeep, *Financial Theory and Corporate Policy*. 4th ed. (Harlow, Essex: Pearson, 2014).

Cunningham, Lawrence A., *The Essays of Warren Buffet: Lessons for Investors and Managers*. 4th ed. (Singapore: John Wiley & Sons Singapore, 2014).

Damodaran, Aswath, *Investment Valuation: Tools and Techniques for Determining the Value of Any Asset*. 3rd ed. (Hoboken, New Jersey: John Wiley & Sons, 2012).

Dobelli, Rolf, *The Art of Thinking Clearly* (London: Sceptre, 2013).

Dorsey, Patrick, *The Five Rules for Successful Stock Investing: Morningstar's Guide to Building Wealth and Winning in the Market* (Hoboken, New Jersey: John Wiley & Sons, 2004).

Dorsey, Patrick, *The Little Book that Builds Wealth: The Knockout Formula for Finding Great Investments* (Hoboken, New Jersey: John Wiley & Sons, 2008).

Duhigg, Charles, *The Power of Habit: Why We Do What We Do and How to Change* (London: Random House Books, 2013).

Fisher, Philip A., *Common Stocks and Uncommon Profits and Other Writings* (Hoboken, New Jersey: John Wiley & Sons, 2003).

Graham, Benjamin, *The Intelligent Investor* (New York: HarperCollins Publishers, 2003).

Grant, Robert M., *Contemporary Strategy Analysis*. 5th ed. (Oxford: Blackwell Publishing, 2005).

Greene, Robert, *The 48 Laws of Power* (London: Profile Books, 2000).

Greenwald, Bruce C. N. and Kahn, Judd, *Competition Demystified: A Radically Simplified Approach to Business Strategy* (New York: Portfolio, 2007).

Greenwald, Bruce C. N., Kahn, Judd, Sonkin, Paul D., and van Biema, Michael, *Value Investing: From Graham to Buffet and beyond* (Hoboken, New Jersey: John Wiley & Sons, 2001).

Hagstrom, Robert G., *The Warren Buffet Way*. 2nd ed. (Hoboken, New Jersey: John Wiley & Sons, 2005).

Hammond, P. Brett Jr., Leibowitz, Martin L., and Siegel, Laurence B., *Rethinking the Equity Risk Premium* (USA: Research Foundation of CFA Institute, 2011).

Harford, Tim, *The Undercover Economist* (Great Britain: Abacus, 2007).

Hill, Napoleon, *Think and Grow Rich* (London: Vermilion, 2004).

Horan, Stephen M., Johnson, Robert R., and Robinson, Thomas R., *Strategic Value Investing: Practical Techniques of Leading Value Investors* (USA: McGraw-Hill Education, 2014).

Hoskisson, Robert E., Hitt, Michael A., and Ireland, R. Duane, *Competing for Advantage* (Mason, Ohio: Thomson South-Western, 2004).

Kahneman, Daniel, *Thinking, Fast and Slow* (London: Penguin Books, 2012).

Kaplan, Robert S. and Norton, David P., *The Strategy-Focused Organization: How Balanced Scorecard Companies Thrive in the New Business Environment* (Boston: Harvard Business School Press, 2001).

Koch, Richard, *Living the 80 / 20 Way: Work Less, Worry Less, Succeed More, Enjoy More* (London: Nicholas Brealey Publishing, 2004).

Koller, Tim, Dobbs, Richard, and Huyett, Bill, *Value: The Four Cornerstones of Corporate Finance* (Hoboken, New Jersey: John Wiley & Sons, 2011).

Koller, Tim, Goedhart, Marc, and Wessels, David, *Valuation: Measuring and Managing the Value of Companies* (Hoboken, New Jersey: John Wiley & Sons, 2010).

Lefèvre, Edwin, *Reminiscences of a Stock Operator* (Hoboken, New Jersey: John Wiley & Sons, 1994).

Loewenstein, George, *Exotic Preferences: Behavioural Economics and Human Motivation* (New York: Oxford University Press, 2007).

Magretta, Joan, *Understanding Michael Porter: The Essential Guide to Competition and Strategy* (Boston: Harvard Business Review Press, 2012).

Marks, Howard, *The Most Important Thing Illuminated: Uncommon Sense for the Thoughtful Investor* (New York: Columbia University Press, 2013).

Menger, Carl, *Principles of Economics* (USA: Skyler J. Collins, 2012).

Montier, James, *Value Investing: Tools and Techniques for Intelligent Investment* (Chichester, West Sussex: John Wiley & Sons, 2009).

Morin, Roger A. and Jarrell, Sherry L., *Driving Shareholder Value: Value-Building Techniques for Creating Shareholder Wealth* (London: McGraw-Hill, 2001).

Osterwalder, Alexander and Pigneur, Yves, *Business Model Generation: A Handbook for Visionaries, Game Changers, and Challengers* (Hoboken, New Jersey: John Wiley & Sons, 2010).

Payne, Oliver, *Inspiring Sustainable Behaviour: 19 Ways to Ask for Change* (New York: Routledge, 2012).

Parameswaran, M. G., *Building Brand Value: Five Steps to Building Powerful Brands* (New Delhi: Tata McGraw-Hill, 2006).

Penman, Stephen, *Accounting for Value* (New York: Columbia University Press, 2011).

Porter, Michael E., *Competitive Advantage: Creating and Sustaining Superior Performance* (New York: Free Press, 2004).

Porter, Michael E., *Competitive Strategy: Techniques for Analysing Industries and Competitors* (New York: Free Press, 2004).

Rajan, Raghuram G. and Zingales, Luigi, *Saving Capitalism from the Capitalists: Unleashing the Power of Financial Markets to Create Wealth and Spread Opportunity* (New Jersey: Princeton University Press, 2004).

Rappaport, Alfred, *Creating Shareholder Value: A Guide for Managers and Investors* (New York: The Free Press, 1998).

Ries, Al and Ries, Laura, *The Origin of Brands: How Product Evolution Creates Endless Possibilities for New Brands* (New York: HarperCollins Publishers, 2004).

Rivkin, Steve and Sutherland, Fraser, *The Making of a Name: The Inside Story of the Brands We Buy* (New York: Oxford University Press, 2004).

Shearn, Michael, *The Investment Checklist: The Art of In-Depth Research* (Hoboken, New Jersey: John Wiley & Sons, 2012).

Smith, Adam, *The Money Game* (New York: Random House, 1976).

Stovall, Sam, *The Seven Rules of Wall Street: Cash-Tested Investment Strategies that Beat the Market* (New York: McGraw-Hill, 2009).

Taleb, Nassim Nicholas, *Fooled by Randomness: The Hidden Role of Chance in Life and in the Markets* (London: Penguin Books, 2007).

Thaler, Richard H. and Sunstein, Cass R., *Nudge: Improving Decisions about Health, Wealth, and Happiness* (New York: Penguin Books, 2009).

Viguerie, Patrick, Smit, Sven, and Baghai, Mehrdad, *The Granularity of Growth: How to Identify the Sources of Growth and Drive Enduring Company Performance* (Hoboken, New Jersey: John Wiley & Sons, 2008).

Welch, Jack and Welch, Suzy, *Winning* (New York: Harper, 2005).

Wing, R. L., *The Art of Strategy: A New Translation of Sun Tzu's Classic "The Art of War"* (New York: Broadway Books, 2000).

Information Sources from the Internet:

http://www.aboutmcdonalds.com

http://www.adidas.com

http://www.conocophillips.com

http://www.dow.com

http://www.dupont.com

http://www.iea.org

http://www.kraftheinzcompany.com

http://www.lafargeholcim.com

http://www.monsanto.com

http://www.nike.com

http://www.opec.org

http://www.pepsico.com

http://www.potashcorp.com

http://www.praxair.com

http://www.ses.com

http://www.the-linde-group.com

https://www.barry-callebaut.com

https://www.basf.com

https://www.microsoft.com

https://www.vopak.com

https://www.wellsfargo.com

About the Author

Thomas Lenz is a business analyst and process consultant at Oiltanking, an international, privately owned company in the business field of oil and gas handling and storage; he is currently located in Mumbai, India.

Before joining Oiltanking in 2010, he functioned in the banking sector as an equity portfolio manager. His broad and deep expertise about strategy, business and financial analysis also stems from practical know-how he gained when working for several years at the audit and management consulting company KPMG.

Lenz holds a master of science in economics (MScEc) from the University of Münster, Germany. Besides this, he holds a Chartered Financial Analyst® (CFA®) designation. In addition, Lenz is a Certified Internal Auditor® (CIA®) as well as a Certified IFRS Group Accountant.

In his role as an investment consultant and portfolio manager, Lenz helps individuals and companies all over the world to make better investment decisions and to develop financial wealth.

Professional, comprehensive investment surveys, along with his fully elaborated valuation system and a corresponding investment rationale statement, are available on request.

Contact:
Thomas Lenz
TLInvest@gmx.de

List of Abbreviations

Aka – Also known as

CAPM – Capital asset pricing model

CFA® – Chartered Financial Analyst®

CIA® – Certified Internal Auditor®

EAT – Earnings after taxes

EBT – Earnings before taxes

EBIT – Earnings before interests and taxes

EBITDA – Earnings before interests, taxes, depreciation and amortization

Ed. – Edition

e.g. – exempli gratia

EMH – Efficient market hypothesis

FCFE – Free cash flow to equity

FCFF – Free cash flow to the firm

i.e. – id est

IFRS – International financial reporting standards

NOPAT – Net operating profit after taxes

NPV – Net present value

OPEC – The organization of the petroleum exporting countries

R&D – Research and development

ROE – Return on equity

ROIC – Return on invested capital

RONIC – Return on new invested capital

WACC – Weighted average costs of capital

www.ingramcontent.com/pod-product-compliance
Lightning Source LLC
Chambersburg PA
CBHW070228190526
45169CB00001B/122